Hegel

Studies in Continental Thought

Martin Heidegger

Hegel

1. NEGATIVITY.
A CONFRONTATION WITH HEGEL
APPROACHED FROM NEGATIVITY
(1938–39, 1941)

2. ELUCIDATION OF THE
"INTRODUCTION" TO HEGEL'S
"PHENOMENOLOGY OF SPIRIT"
(1942)

Translated by
Joseph Arel and
Niels Feuerhahn

Indiana University Press
Bloomington and Indianapolis

This book is a publication of

Indiana University Press
Office of Scholarly Publishing
Herman B Wells Library 350
1320 East 10th Street
Bloomington, Indiana 47405 USA

iupress.indiana.edu

Published in German as Martin Heidegger *Gesamtausgabe 68: Hegel: 1. Die Negativität. Eine Auseinandersetzung mit Hegel aus dem Ansatz in der Negativität (1938/39, 1941); 2. Erläuterung der "Einleitung" zu Hegels "Phänomenologie des Geistes" (1942)*, ed. Ingrid Schüßler
© 2009 by Vittorio Klostermann GmbH, Frankfurt am Main

English Translation © 2015 by Indiana University Press

Manufactured in the United States of America

Library of Congress Cataloging-in-Publication Data

Heidegger, Martin, 1889–1976.
[Works. Selections English]
Hegel / Martin Heidegger ; translated by Joseph Arel and Niels Feuerhahn.
pages cm. — (Studies in continental thought)
Includes bibliographical references.
ISBN 978-0-253-01757-4 (hardback : alk. paper) — ISBN 978-0-253-01778-9 (ebook) 1. Negativity (Philosophy) 2. Hegel, Georg Wilhelm Friedrich, 1770–1831. Phänomenologie des Geistes. I. Heidegger, Martin, 1889–1976. Negativität. English. II. Heidegger, Martin, 1889–1976. Erläuterung der "Einleitung" zu Hegels "Phänomenologie des Geistes. English. III. Title.
B3279.H48N4413 2015
193—dc23
2015008173

1 2 3 4 5 20 19 18 17 16 15

CONTENTS

ELUCIDATION OF THE "INTRODUCTION" TO HEGEL'S
"PHENOMENOLOGY OF SPIRIT" (1942)

Translators' Introduction

This is a translation of Martin Heidegger's *Hegel,* which was originally published in German as volume 68 of Heidegger's *Gesamtausgabe* in 1993. This volume comprises two different works: The first, shorter part of the volume has the original title of *Die Negativität. Eine Auseinandersetzung mit Hegel aus dem Ansatz in der Negativität (1938–39, 1941).* The second part bears the title *Erläuterung der "Einleitung" zu Hegels "Phänomenologie des Geistes"(1942).* Though the text, especially the first part, is fragmentary and much less polished than many of his other texts, Heidegger seems to have considered it especially important. As the editor of the German original notes, it was Heidegger himself who grouped the two treatises together and assigned them to a special volume on Hegel. It was also Heidegger himself who assigned both treatises to the third division of the *Gesamtausgabe.* At the time of its publication it was the second volume to come out under the third division of the *Gesamtausgabe:* "Unpublished Treatises: Addresses— Ponderings." The first volume to appear under this division was *Beiträge zur Philosophie (Vom Ereignis),* whose first edition was published in 1989.

In addition to giving some priority to these texts in the organization of his works, Heidegger also explains Hegel's importance quite explicitly. Early on in the first part, he writes, "The singularity of Hegel's philosophy consists *primarily* in the fact that there is no longer a *higher* standpoint of self-consciousness of spirit beyond it. Thus any future, *still* higher standpoint over against it, which would be superordinate to Hegel's system—in the manner by which Hegel's philosophy for its part and in accord with its point of view had to subordinate every previous philosophy—is once and for all impossible" (p.3). Though Heidegger's writing and lectures on Hegel, as well as on the German Idealism of Fichte and Schelling, increased significantly during the period in which this volume takes place, his insistence on Hegel's importance is not new. Many years earlier, in 1915, Heidegger writes that Hegel's philosophy contains "the system of a historical worldview which is most powerful with regard to its fullness, its depth, its conceptuality, and the richness of its experiences, and which as such has removed and surpassed all preceding fundamental philosophical problems." It is the task of philosophy, he continues, "to confront Hegel."[1]

---

1. GA 1: 410–11. Two writers who have written on Heidegger's lectures on negativity in English are Dahlstrom and de Boer. See Daniel O. Dahlstrom,

Heidegger engages in two such confrontations in the present volume, though this was not his first and would not be his last. In section 82 of *Being and Time*,[2] some twelve years after Heidegger claimed that such a confrontation was needed, he addresses Hegel with respect to the relationship between time and spirit. Hegel is one of the philosophers whom Heidegger confronted repeatedly and extensively throughout his life. Heidegger taught a seminar on Hegel's *Logic* as early as 1925–26. In the summer of 1929 he gave a lecture course on German Idealism at the University of Freiburg in which he devoted himself to the philosophies of Fichte, Schelling, and Hegel, although Fichte figures most prominently in the course. The lecture course was published as *Der deutsche Idealismus (Fichte, Schelling, Hegel) und die philosophische Problemlage der Gegenwart* (GA28) in 1997. The lecture course was accompanied by a seminar devoted to the "Preface" of Hegel's *Phenomenology of Spirit* (published as part of GA86, *Seminare: Hegel—Schelling*). One can also look to Heidegger's lectures at the University of Freiburg on the *Phenomenology of Spirit* in the winter semester of 1930–31,[3] and "Hegel's Concept of Experience,"[4] which was written shortly after the second part of this volume, or to important later works like the 1957 essay "The Onto-theological Constitution of Metaphysics," which is based on a seminar that Heidegger taught on Hegel's *Science of Logic,* or the 1958 lecture "Hegel and the Greeks."[5]

As the presence of direct addresses to an audience that can be found in both parts of "Hegel" indicates, the occasion for the composition of both treatises was likely their oral presentation to an audience. As the editor of the German original explains in her afterword, Heidegger may have presented or at least intended to present both treatises to

"Thinking of Nothing: Heidegger's Criticism of Hegel's Conception of Negativity," in *A Companion to Hegel,* ed. Stephen Houlgate and Michael Baur (Malden, Mass.: Wiley-Blackwell, 2011), and Karin de Boer, *Thinking in the Light of Time: Heidegger's Encounter with Hegel* (Albany: SUNY Press, 2000).

2. Martin Heidegger, *Being and Time,* trans. John Macquarrie and Edward Robinson (New York: Harper & Row, 1962).

3. Martin Heidegger, *Hegel's Phenomenology of Spirit,* trans. Parvis Emad and Kenneth Maly (Bloomington: Indiana University Press, 1980). This lecture course was published in 1980 as volume 32 of the *Gesamtausgabe* under the title *Hegels Phänomenologie des Geistes* and came out in an English translation in 1988.

4. Cf. Martin Heidegger, *Holzwege, Gesamtausgabe,* Band 5 (Frankfurt: Vittorio Klostermann Verlag, 1977), 115–208. "Hegel's Concept of Experience," in *Off the Beaten Track* (Cambridge University Press, 2002), 86–156.

5. Cf. Martin Heidegger, *Wegmarken, Gesamtausgabe,* Band 9 (Frankfurt: Vittorio Klostermann Verlag, 1976), 427–444. "Hegel and the Greeks," in *Pathmarks* (Cambridge: Cambridge University Press, 1998), 323–336.

a (small) circle of colleagues. Given the fragmentary and sketch-like character of "Negativity," it is unclear whether Heidegger ever presented the reflections on Hegel's negativity in the form in which they can be found in "Negativity." The specificity of the address at the beginning of "Negativity," where Heidegger told his audience that the discussion of Hegel's negativity "should not interrupt the course of your work of interpreting Hegel's *Logic*" (p.3) suggests that Heidegger had a particular audience in mind when he composed "Negativity," even if he never actually presented his reflections to this audience.

Aside from the difference in length, one striking difference between parts one and two of *Hegel* is the difference in style and in their respective degree of elaboration of the two treatises. The first part contains at times an elliptical and fragmentary style. As the German editor notes, this fragmentary and sketch-like style character of much of "Negativity" gives the reader an insight into the process of Heidegger's questioning and thinking. The second part, in contrast, displays a much greater degree of elaboration and stylistic cohesion. The differences between the two parts in terms of the respective arrangement of the material are equally striking. After a "preliminary consideration," the second part follows the structure of the "Introduction" of the *Phenomenology of Spirit*. The first part, in contrast, does not have a comparable linear structure. Its first section, titled "Negativity. Nothing—abyss—beyng" comprises thirty-four pages in the German original and is longer than the other four sections combined. The significant length and the comprehensiveness of the material treated suggest a certain priority of this section. The next three sections do not go beyond the ideas found in the first section, but rather elaborate some of the ideas found therein, while the central ideas of the final section, titled "Hegel," seem to have already been incorporated into the first section. This could suggest that the remarks of this section served as the basis for the more elaborated articulation that constitutes the beginning of the first section of "Negativity."

Heidegger's direct address to his audience at the beginning of the first section is not only the clearest indication that "Negativity" was indeed at least intended for presentation to an audience, but also suggests that the portion of "Negativity" that for us constitutes its first section may in fact have been projected to become the treatise that Heidegger was going to present. If this hypothesis is plausible, then the remaining twenty sub-sections of the first section of "Negativity" can be read as a kind of "outline" of Heidegger's treatise on Hegel's negativity, and despite the fact that much of "Negativity" is not fully elaborated we get a fairly good sense of the shape that Heidegger's treatise on Hegel's negativity may have had in its final version.

Given the outstanding position of Hegel's philosophy in the history of Western metaphysics, if Heidegger is to effect a *Destruktion* of Western metaphysics, as he aims to do throughout much of his work, this project will have to deal with Hegel. Just as Hegel is not an arbitrary philosophical interlocutor for Heidegger, neither is the approach to Hegel's philosophy from negativity arbitrary. It is rather derived from the specificity of Hegel's philosophy and the unique challenges that any *philosophical* confrontation with it faces. Hegel's philosophy is not only uniquely important, but it also poses a unique challenge to those who seek to confront it. This unique challenge stems from the peculiar essence of Hegel's philosophy. That the confrontation with Hegel is undertaken from negativity is due to two fundamental requirements that such a confrontation must satisfy: the confrontation with Hegel, says Heidegger, cannot bring in criticisms that are external to the system. To do so would be to miss the motivating ground for the system itself, and the resulting criticisms would be meritless. Instead of pursuing a still higher standpoint above the Hegelian one, one must adopt a more originary standpoint than the one that Hegel himself adopts, yet one that is not merely imposed on Hegel's thinking from the outside. That is to say, a fundamental confrontation with Hegel's philosophy must adopt a standpoint that at the same times lies in Hegel's philosophy and yet remains "essentially inaccessible and indifferent" (p.4) to it. Furthermore, in order to do justice to the principle of Hegel's philosophy a confrontation with Hegel must grasp that which is fundamental in Hegel's philosophy in its "determinateness and power of determination" (p.5). In short, a fundamental confrontation that seeks to be more than a historiological exposition of Hegel's philosophy must be guided by an essential question.

In part one of "Hegel" Heidegger advances the thesis that the basic determination of Hegelian philosophy that can lead to a more originary standpoint is negativity (cf. p.6). Negativity constitutes the suitable approach for this confrontation with Hegel because a fundamental confrontation with Hegel needs to be guided by an essential question and because "Negativity is questionless both in the system that constitutes the *consummation* of Western metaphysics and in the history of metaphysics in general" (p.31). What Heidegger aims to show in "Negativity" is that although negativity plays a prominent role throughout Hegel's philosophy, Hegel does not take negativity seriously enough and negativity itself does not become a question for him. To say that negativity is not a question for Hegel means that its origin and essential structure are not treated as questionworthy or questionable and thus remain concealed.

It is precisely this concealed origin of negativity that interests Heidegger, because to find the origin of negativity means to attain that standpoint that would allow one to conduct a fundamental confrontation with Hegel that would satisfy the two demands that Heidegger identifies at the beginning of the treatise. What Heidegger sets out to do in "Negativity" is to examine the questionlessness of Hegel's negativity, in terms of both what it means for his philosophy and with respect to its peculiar presuppositions.

For Hegel, "negativity" is the difference of consciousness (cf. p.11). More specifically, it is the threefold difference of unconditioned consciousness (cf. p.29). As such, negativity is the energy of unconditioned thinking, the essence of absolute subjectivity (cf. p.11). Heidegger does not only examine that which Hegel calls negativity, he also looks at Hegel's negativity understood as a realm of inquiry, that is, "the connection of *saying-no, negation, negatedness, not, nothing,* and *nullity*" (p.29). Here it is especially the examination of the nothing that holds the promise to shed light on negativity (cf. p.13). However, what Heidegger finds is that in both cases negativity is completely questionless for Hegel, because the central determination of Hegel's negativity is that it is "one of thinking and thoughtness" (p.17). While Hegel's ultimate aim is to think thought and thoughtness unconditionally, thought itself is self-evident for Hegel; and it is precisely this self-evidence of thought that entails that negativity does not and cannot become a question for Hegel.

Heidegger notes that the questionlessness of negativity does not imply that an inquiry would be altogether futile or impossible. In fact, Heidegger tells us that we must tarry with what is questionless, because that which is questionless is not only that which does not allow for an inquiry but also precisely "that which is at bottom *un*decided but which in the flight from mindfulness passes itself off as something that is decided" (p.30). For Heidegger, Hegel's negativity is questionless in just this ambiguous sense and thus highly questionworthy.

As Heidegger attempts to show, the questionlessness of Hegel's negativity is a consequence of the questionlessness of the essence of thought. Thought, in turn, is self-evident and thus questionless insofar as it is the essential characteristic of man conceived as the rational animal. To ask the question of the origin of negativity, therefore, means to ask what the questionlessness of thought conceived as the basic human capacity signifies and comprises (cf. p.31). Heidegger's approach in confronting Hegel is thus not to go beyond him, but to go back into what he takes to be the concealed ground of his thinking.

In the second part of this volume, Heidegger shifts his focus to Hegel's *Phenomenology of Spirit*. The *Phenomenology*, and with it the "Phenomenology-system," is rooted in experience as its most fundamental ground. Thus, Heidegger aims to explicate Hegel's concept of experience in order to properly confront the motivating ground of Hegel's phenomenological method in the "Phenomenology-system." He does this through a paragraph by paragraph analysis of the "Introduction" to the *Phenomenology of Spirit*.

In the winter semester of 1930–31 Heidegger had given a lecture course on the *Phenomenology of Spirit* at the University of Freiburg. In this lecture course Heidegger omits discussion of both the "Preface" and the "Introduction" and instead devotes himself to the explication of Sections A and B of the *Phenomenology*. In the years following this lecture course Heidegger gave three seminars on Hegel's *Phenomenology of Spirit*.[6] Next to the more comprehensive "Hegel's Concept of Experience," which would be published in 1950 but which is based on seminars that Heidegger taught in 1942–43, part two of *Hegel* offers a glimpse at the evolution of Heidegger's thinking about Hegel's *Phenomenology* since his lecture course in 1930–31.

In part two, called "Elucidation of the 'Introduction' to Hegel's 'Phenomenology of Spirit,'" Heidegger groups the sixteen paragraphs of the "Introduction" into five sections. While the first four sections are worked out in detail, the final section, dealing with paragraph 16 of the "Introduction," consists of eighteen numbered "sketches." Of these five sections the one dealing with paragraphs 14 and 15 is by far the longest. The title of that section is "The Essence of the Experience of Consciousness and Its Presentation." The primacy of this topic can hardly surprise us if we recall that the original subtitle of the work that would later become known as *Science of the Phenomenology of Spirit* or, in short, *Phenomenology of Spirit*, was *Science of the Experience of Consciousness*, a title that is a constant interest for Heidegger, and whose disappearance, Heidegger concedes, ultimately remains something of a mystery. The centrality of the concept of experience for any confrontation with Hegel's philosophy is further attested by the fact that in 1950 Heidegger published a separate essay titled "Hegel's Concept of Experience." In addition to the discussion of the proper starting point for philosophy, and Hegel's starting point in particular, the 1942–43 essay also gives a paragraph by paragraph analysis of the "Introduction" of the *Phenomenology of Spirit*.[7] What the reader will find in the analysis of experience found in this volume is Heidegger's continuing

---

6. These seminars are all published in volume 86 of the *Gesamtausgabe*.
7. This essay was published as a part of *Off the Beaten Track* in 1977.

attempt to outline the grounds for assessing the true impact of Hegel's philosophy, an analysis of the role of the *Phenomenology* within Hegel's philosophical system, an insightful and rigorous analysis of what exactly experience is, with reference to the history of philosophy (in particular, to Kant and Aristotle), and, importantly, the ways in which Hegel's conception of experience presents us with important advances and insights into how we should properly approach philosophical investigations.

Notes on the Translation

The difficulties of translating the works of Martin Heidegger into English are well known and have been well noted. Overall we have tried to situate our translation in the context of the rich Heidegger literature. We have attempted to abstain from any unnecessary neologisms and have in many cases adopted what appeared to us to be the most plausible existing translation of a given word. While we have explained some specific translation choices in the text itself, in this introduction we want to mention some of the more general choices that we have made:

1. Hyphenation: The hyphenations that Heidegger employs frequently throughout *Hegel* cannot always intelligibly be rendered into English. As a general rule we have tried to preserve Heidegger's hyphens wherever plausible. This was achieved most successfully where the etymology of the English word is sufficiently similar to that of the German. We are able to follow Heidegger's hyphenations with words like "de-cision" (*Ent-scheidung*), "dis-illusionment" (*Ent-täuschung*), "dismantling" (*Ab-bau*), "pre-dilection" (*Vor-liebe*), and "question-worthy" (*frag-würdig*). In the majority of cases, however, differences in etymology did not allow for a plausible adoption of Heidegger's hyphenations. Where this is the case we have not replicated Heidegger's hyphenation in the English word but have included the hyphenated German word in brackets instead. This applies both to words that could be hyphenated in English but would have a meaning that differs from the one that Heidegger's own hyphenation is meant to convey and to words in English that allow for no meaningful hyphenation based on the semantics of the word in question. To the former category belongs the word "*Erfahrung*," which Heidegger sometimes renders as "*Er-fahrung*." Since the meaning of the prefix "ex-" is not the same as that which "*er-*" has in German it would be misleading and would ultimately misrepresent Heidegger's German to hyphenate the word. Examples of words where the etymology of the English term allowed

for no possible hyphenation at all include "origin," which in German Heidegger sometimes writes as "*Ur-sprung*," as well as the word "difference" when rendered by Heidegger as "*Unter-schied*." We have chosen to exempt certain words from this rule that are well-established in the English-speaking Heidegger literature. Words like "a-byss" (*Ab-grund*), "e-vent" (*Er-eignis*), "re-nunciation" (*Ab-sage*), and "re-presentation" (*Vor-stellen*) have become part of the Heidegger lexicon and have been adopted, though the words have no meaningful connection in terms of their respective etymologies. In those cases where we have translated Heidegger's terms with the help of two separate words, for example, "regressive inquiry" for "*Zurück-fragen*," and "leaping attainment" for "*Er-springung*," we have also included the German word in brackets.

One of the more difficult hyphenations in *Hegel* is the word "*Bewußt-sein*." With one exception, we have translated "*Bewußtsein*," when used without a hyphen, as "consciousness." Where Heidegger writes "*Bewußt-sein*" we have on all but one occasion translated this as "being-conscious." Where we deviate from this translation, "*Bewußt-sein*" is rendered as "being an object of consciousness." Another word that deserves special mention is "*Vorstellen*." In the majority of cases we have translated "*Vorstellen*" and its derivatives as "representation." Where we felt that Heidegger placed a special emphasis on the literal sense of "*vor-stellen*," ("*vor*" meaning "out in front of" and "*stellen*" meaning "to place, make stand, or put") graphically expressed by the hyphenation of the word, we have translated it as "placing-before," or "placing-before-oneself" for "*Vor-sich-stellen*."

2. Heidegger's use of quotation marks: As the editor of the German text notes, Heidegger makes ample use of underlining and quotation marks, all of which were preserved in the German edition in order to reflect the "author's style of work" (cf. "Editor's Afterword"). We have tried to preserve these quotation marks whenever plausible. Some of these quotation marks clearly refer to titles of published works. For example, all references to Kant's "Kritik der reinen Vernunft" refer to Kant's book with the same title and are thus rendered in italics. The greatest challenge was posed by the phrases "*Phänomenologie des Geistes*," the shortened version "*Phänomenologie*," and the long version "*Wissenschaft der Phänomenologie des Geistes*." In the majority of cases the phrases refer to Hegel's text and are thus written in italics and capitalized. Heidegger also refers to the introduction and preface of Hegel's *Phenomenology of Spirit* concisely as "'Preface'" or "'Introduction.'" There are instances in which Heidegger speaks about the preface or introduction of the *Phenomenology* without placing these terms in quotation marks. In order to be as faithful to the original German as possible we

have adopted this on the assumption that this distinction is deliberate. Whether it is in all cases *plausible* is a separate matter that we leave for the reader to decide. Lastly, as other translators have noted with respect to other texts by Heidegger, Heidegger does not always indicate when he is talking about a book. For instance, the phrase "phenomenology of spirit" can also refer to the philosophical work done, and not the book written by Hegel. There are some instances in *Hegel* where Heidegger does not indicate that he is referring to a work even though the context makes any other interpretation implausible. In these cases we have added the appropriate formatting even though it does not appear in the German original.

3. Quotations from the *Phenomenology of Spirit* and other works: The present volume contains quotations from several works by Hegel, first and foremost the *Phenomenology of Spirit* and *The Science of Logic*. In order to maintain terminological consistency throughout this translation we have retranslated all passages from the *Phenomenology of Spirit* and *The Science of Logic* that appear in the present volume. In doing this we have greatly benefited from the work of A. V. Miller, George di Giovanni, and other translators of the writings of Hegel and Heidegger. We would like to acknowledge our indebtedness to them. For quotations from all other works by Hegel we have reproduced the translation as it can be found in the standard English translations of the respective work. Where we modified an existing translation, we have noted this in the corresponding footnote. Latin or Greek sources quoted by Heidegger in this volume were rendered following Heidegger's own translations of these sources. This was done in order to retain the specific meaning that Heidegger gives to the original sentence or phrase, a meaning that could have easily been lost if we had only reproduced an English translation of the Latin or Greek original. In the corresponding footnote we have also provided the English translation of the original passage as it appears in an existing English translation of the primary text quoted by Heidegger.

4. We have included the original citations as they appear in the German edition. When these citations refer to *Hegel's Werke: Vollständige Ausgabe durch einen Verein von Freunden des Verewigten* (19 vols. Berlin, 1832–45 and 1887), we have followed the convention of referring to the edition by the abbreviation "WW" with a Roman numeral for the volume. We have furthermore included the page numbers in the English translation of the original works. For the *Phänomenologie des Geistes* we refer to the paragraph numbers from A. V. Miller's translation, which appears under the title *Hegel's Phenomenology of Spirit* (Oxford: Oxford University Press, 1977). For the *Wissenschaft der Logik* we refer to G. di Giovanni's translation, which appears under the title

The Science of Logic (Cambridge: Cambridge University Press, 2010). In the footnotes we refer to these editions as *"Phenomenology"* and *"Science of Logic"* respectively. Bibliographical information for all other works that are cited in *Hegel* can be found in the footnotes to the corresponding quotation.

5. We have attempted to preserve the greatest possible terminological consistency both within the individual parts and between them. As such we have tried to avoid, as much as possible, using the same English word to translate two different key terms, even if different English words would have offered the most desirable English term in each case when taken individually. The practice is complicated by the fact that there are certain German words of an ambiguous semantic wealth that no single English word can simply reproduce. For example, the word *"Einfall"* (literally "fall into") can mean, and is used by Heidegger at times in these two senses, both "mere idea" and "intrusion." We have translated the term *"Einfall"* for the most part as "mere idea" and occasionally as "intrusion" when Heidegger emphasizes the moment of (forcefully) entering into from outside. When the adjectival form *"einfallend"* is used, we have translated it as "incidental," following di Giovanni's translation of *"einfallende Reflexion"* as "incidental reflection." In all these cases, the glossary will clearly indicate the different translations that correspond to the same German word.

6. "To undergo an experience": In part two of *Hegel* the phrase *"eine Erfahrung machen"* comes up numerous times. We have translated the standard German expression *"eine Erfahrung machen"* (literally "to make an experience") by "to undergo an experience." It should be noted that in relation to "undergo," the German *"machen"* has a more active connotation. The phrases *"eine Erfahrung an etwas machen"* and *"eine Erfahrung über etwas machen"* have generally been translated by "to undergo an experience with something" and "to undergo an experience of something," respectively.

7. Especially throughout "Negativity," Heidegger's writing style is often elliptical. Many times Heidegger will omit the appropriate inflection of "to be." For the most part, this does not render the content more obscure. As such it would have been just as easy to fill in copulas or articles that are missing in the German edition in order to increase the flow of the text as it would have been redundant given the readability of Heidegger's treatise. We have for the most part refrained from compensating Heidegger's elliptical style, except in those instances where an equally elliptical English translation would have failed to afford the same comprehensibility as the German original. Given the ubiquity of Heidegger's elliptical style, filling in the appropriate words would have significantly altered the overall appearance

of the text and would have suggested to the English reader a much more "polished" manuscript than the original actually is.

8. Lastly, we have included a comprehensive glossary at the end of this volume in order to make our translation as transparent as possible.

Two notes on the technical aspects of the translation: First, the numbering of the footnotes in the German original differs between "Negativity" and "Elucidation of the 'Introduction' to Hegel's *Phenomenology of Spirit*." In the former, the footnotes are numbered consecutively from the beginning of each subsection. In part two, in contrast, the footnotes are numbered consecutively from the beginning of each of the five main sections. Secondly, all of the additions that in the original text appeared in square brackets, whether those be Heidegger's own (e.g., when he quotes Hegel) or those of the editor, appear in curly brackets { } in this translation. All additions to the German text by the translators of this volume are within square brackets [ ]. In addition to the original footnotes that can be found in the German text, this translation contains additional endnotes by the translators of this volume. Superscripted notes in brackets indicate a translators' note.

Finally, we would like to thank Kenneth Maly for help at the beginning stages of the translation, our external reviewer for helpful suggestions, Dee Mortensen at Indiana University Press, and our copy editor, Carol Kennedy.

Hegel

NEGATIVITY.
A CONFRONTATION WITH HEGEL
APPROACHED FROM NEGATIVITY

(1938–39, 1941)

I. NEGATIVITY.
NOTHING—ABYSS—BEYNG

1. On Hegel

The explorations that we are attempting in the form of a discussion should not interrupt the course of your work of interpreting Hegel's *Logic*. The questions that we are striving toward are also not intended to "intrude on" Hegel's philosophy from the outside with the "impatience of incidental reflection,"[1] which is thoroughly contrary to a system of thinking, particularly of the Hegelian type, and must therefore also be fruitless.

It is also true that Hegel does not simply serve us as an arbitrary opportunity and foothold for a philosophical confrontation. His philosophy *stands* definitively in the history of thinking—or should we say: of beyng—as the singular and not yet comprehended *demand* for a confrontation with it. This demand holds for any thinking that comes *after* it or for any thinking that simply wants to—and perhaps must—prepare again for philosophy.

Nietzsche, who freed himself very slowly and rather late from the pathetic slander and disregard for Hegel that he inherited from Schopenhauer, once said that "we Germans are Hegelians, even if there had never been a Hegel."[2]

The singularity of Hegel's philosophy consists *primarily* in the fact that there is no longer a *higher* standpoint of self-consciousness of spirit beyond it. Thus any future, *still* higher standpoint over against it, which would be superordinate to Hegel's system—in the manner

---

1. G. W. F. Hegel, *Wissenschaft der Logik*, ed. Georg Lasson (Leipzig, 1923). Preface to the second edition, 21. [*Science of Logic*, 21.]

2. Cf. Friedrich Nietzsche, *Die Fröhliche Wissenschaft*. Book V, 357. *Großoktavausgabe*, vol. 5, 230. [English: *The Gay Science*, trans. Josefine Nauckhoff (Cambridge: Cambridge University Press, 2001), 218; translation modified.]

by which Hegel's philosophy for its part and in accord with its point of view had to subordinate every previous philosophy—is once and for all impossible.

All the same, if the standpoint of a necessary confrontation with Hegel's philosophy is to be on equal footing with it, and that means of course that it is in an essential respect superior to it, while at the same time not brought to and forced on it from the outside, then this standpoint of the confrontation must in fact lie concealed *in* Hegel's philosophy—as its own essentially inaccessible and indifferent ground. However, that and why the standpoint of Schelling's late philosophy may in no way be taken up as a standpoint superior to Hegel shall not be dealt with here.[3]

In view of the uniqueness of the standpoint of his philosophy, the confrontation with Hegel is also subject to unique conditions. It has nothing in common with any sort of "critique," that is, an account of what is incorrect, which would be derived from applying the standards of preceding standpoints or of earlier standpoints that, in the meantime, have been revised—for instance, those of Kantianism, Medieval-Scholasticism, or Cartesianism.

The other thing that a fundamental confrontation with Hegel needs to be mindful of originates in something that Hegel claimed as the distinguishing mark of his system very early on, and again and again afterward: that the standpoint of his philosophy is actually elaborated and that the principle of his philosophy across all areas (nature, art, law, state, religion) is pursued and presented throughout. Philosophy that comes after Hegel cannot be content with merely having a "knack" for a new kind of wisdom;[4] the principle must show itself in the totality of beings and must thus validate this totality as actuality. "True thoughts and scientific insight are only to be won in the labor of the concept. The concept alone can bring forth the universality of knowledge, which is neither the common indeterminacy and inadequacy of common sense, but rather well-formed and complete cognition, nor the uncommon universality of the capacity of reason, which corrupts itself through sluggishness and conceit of genius, but rather

---

3. Cf. seminar WS 1937–38, *Die Grundstellungen der abendländischen Metaphysik.* {The notes of the seminar will be published in the volumes of the seminars of the fourth division of the *Gesamtausgabe.*} [The notes of the seminars were published as *Die metaphysischen Grundstellungen des abendländischen Denkens* and constitute part one of the volume *Seminare (Übungen) 1937–38 und 1941–42* (GA88).]

4. Cf. G. W. F. Hegel, *Phänomenologie des Geistes,* ed. Johannes Hoffmeister (Leipzig, 1937). Preface, 43. [*Phenomenology,* §51.]

a truth ripened to its properly matured form so as to be capable of being the property of all self-conscious reason."[5]

Whether in fact the elaboration of the principle of the system, as Hegel demands it, holds for all philosophy in general or only for the kind of systematic philosophy of German Idealism, and also, what this demand means in altered form for another inquiry, cannot be discussed here. But in any case, a fundamental confrontation with Hegel, one that is directed at the principle and standpoint, risks that by grasping merely the principle it grasps precisely that—or not even that—which remains empty and indeterminate and is not the intended philosophy itself.

From this we may infer that a fundamental confrontation with Hegel's philosophy that is adequate to it as a whole can be achieved *only* in a way that follows every step of Hegel's thinking in every area of his system.

But what would be achieved here other than, generally speaking, always only the presentation of the same principle, albeit in a different penetrability and illuminatory force depending on the area in question (art, religion)? This would certainly not be an insignificant achievement—and *yet would never be* what is *decisive*. On the other hand, the detached discussion of the empty principle and of the meager skeleton of the form of the system are prohibited because they do not make manifest the *being-principle of the principle*.

In line with these considerations, every fundamental confrontation with Hegel stands or falls depending on whether it satisfies, *at the same time* and *in a unified manner,* these *two* demands: first, to occupy a more originary standpoint, one that does not intrude from outside, and on the other hand, to grasp in an originary manner what is fundamental in its determinateness and power of determination, while avoiding both the depletion of the principle of the system and a merely formalistic discussion of it as it can be found in the usual—historiological—expositions, that is, in those that are *not* guided by an essential question.

Where then does the critical meditation have to begin in order to satisfy this twofold demand? What is that basic determination of Hegel's philosophy that we must think through in order to be led back into a more originary standpoint from which alone we can truly catch

---

5. Ibid., 57. Cf. Hegel's letter to von Raumer 1816: "Über den Vortrag der Philosophie auf Universitäten." WW XVII, 351f. [*Phenomenology,* §70. An English translation of the letter to von Raumer appears in *Hegel: The Letters,* trans. Clark Butler and Christiane Seiler (Bloomington: Indiana University Press, 1984), 337–341.]

sight of it as a basic determination? And what is this basic determination that at the same time does justice to that which the Hegelian system has worked through?

We claim: this basic determination is *"negativity."* However, before we move on to a closer characterization of Hegelian negativity, some prior questions need to be sorted out.

(1) The clarification of a concern regarding the value of such a confrontation.

(2) The specification of the conceptual language that comes into play in the confrontation.

(3) The preliminary characterization of the standpoint and principle of Hegel's philosophy.

(1) Clarification of a concern regarding the value of such a confrontation

It can be doubted whether Hegel's philosophy still has an impact today, so that it seems that the confrontation with it, regardless of how much it is concerned with what is fundamental, remains after all only a scholarly game of the usual philosophical-historical *historicism,* one that is, as we say, concerned with the "history of ideas"—a making-present of Hegelian philosophy as a past one in which many curiosities may be noticed and which, if it is conducted thoroughly enough, perhaps contributes to the sharpening of the understanding. This doubt, namely whether such a historicism is and can be more than a scholarly occupation, expresses the opinion that the actual relevance of a philosophy consists in its effects or after-effects. As if Hegel's philosophy would only actually be relevant today if there were a Hegelianism and to the extent that it existed in fact in various forms! That a philosophy produces a school and that this school in turn practices a "philology" and a learnedness *about* the philosophy in question, this is indeed an effect of the philosophy—and one that is for the most part an irrelevant effect; this effect, however, never contains that which the philosophy in question *is* historically *from itself* and *in itself.*

The actual relevance of Hegelian philosophy also does not lend itself to be measured by what it meant for the "life" of its time through its immediate, contemporary influence. What we encounter here is the common view that Hegel's philosophy and German Idealism in general always remained the extravagant speculation of some fanciful minds and thus stood "outside" of so-called "life." To that one must respond that German Idealism as a whole and Hegel's philosophy in particular unfolds a historically effective force whose extent and limits we today cannot yet fathom because we are flooded by it from all directions without recognizing it. However, one must know that this kind of "impact" of a philosophy precisely does not consist in that its doctrines are adopted, "espoused" as they say, carried over into the so-called praxis of "life," and are thereby confirmed and its validity is upheld. The "impact" of a philosophy has an enigmatic thing about it, that in effecting its "time," it calls forth precisely its opposite and compels it to revolt against it. In short: Without German Idealism and without Hegel's metaphysics in particular, the positivism of the nine-teenth century and of our time could never have gained the stability and self-evidence that belongs to it.

The age in which Nietzsche was rooted and caught up is unthink-able without Hegel, not to mention Marx and Marxism, which is, after all, more than just a particular formulation of socialism. But Hegel's metaphysics has a *mere* semblance of actual relevance, namely, in that today's Hegelians band together in order to make themselves timely in the name of Hegel's "concrete" thinking. Hegel still has an impact everywhere today, yet always in a reversal and disguise or, in turn, in the counter-movement against this reversal and disguise. Chris-tian theology of both denominations is determined by Hegel and even more so by the religious-historical theological counter-movements and formations of the ecclesiastical consciousness that grew out of it.[6]

And nevertheless: Even *this* actual relevance of his philosophy, un-derstood as the historical impact proper to it, does *not* constitute what this philosophy as philosophy *is, still is,* and *will be.* With this we in no way think of a supertemporal validity of any "correct" propositions that one wants to find in it among many incorrect, flawed, and obso-lete things. We mean rather "only" this: *that* this philosophy *is,*—that *here* that which philosophy has to think *is* thought in a distinctive manner; that something happens here that does not take place out-side of "time," but indeed has its own time, to the extent that it origi-narily grounds the latter. We may not, neither now nor in the future, measure the *historical* being of a philosophy with the standards of *his-toriology;* the impact and effectivity on so-called life is no possible fac-tor for the judgment of a philosophy, and with it also not for the esti-mation of the worth of a confrontation with it; because all "life" and what is so called "lives" only out of the misrecognition and turning away *from* philosophy,—this means only that it necessarily and in a very embarrassing way needs philosophy. But philosophy can never consider "life's" *turning away* from it a deficiency but must rather know

---

6. "Bankrupt"—"dialectical theology." Catholic theology: crossroad; studies of my time in Freiburg.

it from necessity. *What* and *how* Western philosophy is *historically* cannot be decided by means of historiological considerations but can be experienced only in philosophical thinking.

(2) Specification of the conceptual language
that comes into play in the confrontation

Philosophy is *Western* philosophy;—there is no philosophy other than Western philosophy, inasmuch as the essence of what the West and Western history are is determined by that which is called philosophy. We must abstain from every scholastic conception and every historiological interpretation of philosophy as a cultural phenomenon and instead understand it as the mindfulness of the totality of beings as such, in short—but also again undetermined because ambivalent— *asking the question of being.*

"Being" is the *basic word* of philosophy. What *we* call in this essential, and that means at the same time the initial historical sense, "being," Hegel calls *"actuality"* (compare below). Why exactly *this* designation occurs in Hegel is grounded in the *innermost* essence of the *history* of Western philosophy; why—this will become apparent in our discussion.

In contrast, that which *Hegel* designates with "being" we call "objectness," which is a designation that indeed captures what Hegel himself *also* means. Why Hegel calls "objectness" "being" is, *again*, not arbitrary. It arises from the necessity of a philosophical standpoint that *Hegel himself* must traverse and posit in order to ground *his* philosophy.

Hegel's concept of "actuality"

(According to the preface of the *Elements of the Philosophy of Right.* In the *Logic: "absolute idea";* in the *Phenomenology of Spirit: absolute knowledge,* but also "being.")

Actuality: beingness as representedness of absolute reason. Reason as absolute knowledge—unconditionally re-presenting re-presentation and its representedness.

What is "rational" and what can be called "actual" will be decided *in accordance with this alone.* With this in mind, Hegel's proposition, often quoted and just as often misinterpreted, is to be understood:

"What is rational is actual;
and what is actual is rational."[7]

This proposition is turned into its opposite if by "actual" one understands what is commonly called "actual," that is, the presence-at-

---

7. G. W. F. Hegel, *Grundlinien der Philosophie des Rechts.* Preface. WW VIII, xix (ed. Hoffmeister, 14). [English: *Elements of the Philosophy of Right,* trans. H. B. Nisbet (Cambridge: Cambridge University Press, 1991), 20.]

hand of a contingent "present," and by "reason" the contingent understanding of the self-evidence of common thought.

This proposition is not a determination in the sense of an equation concerning things encountered present-at-hand and a momentarily plausible opinion of the "rational" living creature, called man,—but it is the basic proposition [*Grundsatz*] of the *essential determination of being*. Being is the representedness of unconditionally representing representation (of thinking)—the perceivedness of reason. The proposition is not a practical rule about the assessment of beings, but conveys the essential ground of the *beingness* of beings. The proposition can therefore also not be refuted by the fact that many "rational things" (in the usual {?} sense) do not "happen" and are not "actualized," and thus fail to occur, and that many "actual things" are rather "irrational" (in the sense of calculating understanding). This *essential proposition* cannot be "refuted" whatsoever.

For Hegel, "being" is thus *only a one-sided* determination of that which philosophy, and also Hegelian philosophy, thinks and interrogates: being, in the sense of the question of being as the mindfulness of the totality of beings as such.

Nietzsche, by the way, also uses the basic philosophical word "being" in a *restricted* sense; in fact, this restriction is intimately *related* to Hegel's, not because it is *as a matter of fact* directly borrowed from Hegel's use of language (I suspect that Nietzsche never "read" Hegel's *Logic*, let alone that he ever thought it through in its totality), but rather because both restricted usages of the word "being"—Nietzsche's and Hegel's—have *the same historical* ground, which is none other than the beginning of the history of philosophy and that means of its essence hitherto conceived of as "metaphysics."

In the confrontation with Hegel we must therefore constantly be mindful of whether what is intended is *Hegel's* concept of being or the *essential* concept of being. This is of wide-ranging importance in as much as Hegel brings the "nothing," which is usually considered the negation of beings in general and in their totality, in a decisive conjunction with "being," conceived in its *restricted* sense.—It requires no further emphasis that something completely different than merely "terminological" distinctions is at stake here.

(3) Preliminary characterization of the standpoint and principle of Hegel's philosophy

a) "Standpoint" designates that in which philosophy stands while what is to be thought as such becomes accessible to it, to its thinking. Hegel's standpoint is that of *absolute idealism*. ("Idealism" genuinely and properly only in the modern sense: *idea* as *perceptum* of the *per-*

ceptio as *cogitatio*—as "consciousness.") The standpoint generally that of *consciousness*. Being is re-presentation and re-presentedness of re-presentation; unconditioned subjectivity.

b) "Principle" means that with which philosophy begins, namely such that the *beginning* is that which remains the supporting ground of the thinking of what is to be thought. *Hegel's principle* says: "Substance is subject" or: being (now taken in its essential sense) is "becoming." Hegel begins with the beginning to the extent that for him *to become* is precisely to begin. "Becoming": re-presentation of itself, bringing-itself-to-appearance. In the logic, becoming brings itself into becoming as that which becomes, i.e., in its unconditioned conditions. But is this an absolute determination of the "beginning" and of beginning—or only Hegel's, i.e., the metaphysical determination? The interpretation of the *essence* of "beginning"! From where? With what does Hegel's philosophy proper—the *Logic*—begin? With "becoming"—it is the "ground"; indeed not with "being," this is the *point of departure!* Becoming "is" insofar as it "becomes."

c) To what extent "standpoint and principle" belong together and in what they belong together must ideally be made apparent by the meditation on particular standpoints and principles.

After this short survey of the three preliminary questions, we seek a closer characterization of that wherein our confrontation takes hold— *negativity.*

2. At a glance[1,2,3]

1. The determination of the "standpoint" and the "principle" of Hegelian philosophy; the concepts "standpoint" and "principle." *Standpoint:* absolute idealism, concept of the ab-solute, unconditionedness

---

1. Cf. additions and supplements to *What Is Metaphysics?* {Will be published in one volume of the fourth division of the *Gesamtausgabe: Hinweise zu veröffentlichten Schriften.*}

2. Cf. *Contributions.* {Heidegger, Martin. *Beiträge zur Philosophie (Vom Ereignis) 1936–38, Gesamtausgabe,* vol. 65, ed. F.-W. von Herrmann (Frankfurt a.M.: Klosterman, 1989).} [English: *Contributions to Philosophy (Of the Event),* trans. Richard Rojcewicz and Daniela Vallega-Neu (Bloomington: Indiana University Press, 2000).]

3. Cf. "Beyng" {GA III}, cf. philosophy as confrontation [*Auseinander-setzung*] {GA III}, cf. lecture course on Hegel {GA 32}, and seminars on the *Phenomenology of Spirit,* the *Logic,* and the philosophy of right {GA IV}.—Cf. revised interpretation of Schelling's treatise on freedom, 1941. {Hand-written supplement from the review in 1941.—Cf. GA 49, 105ff.}

of the *ego cogito certum. Principle: Substantiality is subjectivity.* "Being" as "becoming" of absolute knowledge.

2. The characterization of Hegelian "negativity" as *difference* of consciousness. The first question: Whether this difference is drawn from *consciousness* as essence, or whether the characterization as difference is used to determine consciousness (subject-object-relationship), or whether it is both of them and why?

3. The clarification of negativity in the shape of being-other: something and other. The other as the other of the other.

4. Why negativity cannot be determined from Hegel's nothing, since it appears to be the "embodiment" of not-ness; the *nothing* the same as being—neither as differentiated; here still no difference, no negativity.

5. Hegel's concept of "being" arose from the *dis-mantling* of absolute actuality—what is most differentiated from it. The outermost externalization! But absolute actuality as will.

6. Absolute actuality (being in the broader sense) from the *re-nunciation* of the systematic (system-conforming) grounding of the difference between being and beings. This renunciation (already the consummation of neglect) out of the forgetfulness of this distinction. Forgetfulness out of the most habitual habituation to the difference. The dismantling here necessary out of this renunciation; the latter lies in the essence of absolute metaphysics and metaphysics in general: it is and it is being carried out with the enactment of metaphysics.

7. This re-nunciation an essential presupposition of the possible absoluteness of unconditioned thinking.

8. How the complete *dissolution* of negativity into the positivity of the absolute is brought into view from here. "Negativity" is the "energy" of unconditioned thinking because it has from the very beginning already surrendered everything that is negative and not-like. The question of the origin of "negativity" is devoid of sense and ground. Negativity is what is questionless: negativity as the essence of subjectivity. Negativity as the negation of negation is grounded in the yes to unconditioned *self-consciousness*—of absolute certainty as "truth" (i.e., beingness of beings).

9. The questionlessness of negativity as a consequence of the questionlessness of the essence of *thinking.*

10. Thought as the enactment of the representing (as representing itself) determination of beings and as the pregiven horizon of the interpretation of being (perceivedness—presence—thoughtness).

11. The self-evidence of thought as the essential character of man in the sense of the *thinking animal.* Since Descartes the beingness of beings in itself re-presentation. Consciousness as self-consciousness.

12. The questionlessness of negativity and the question of the relation *of man to being* (not only to beings). The proper question of *"anthropomorphism."*

13. Inquiry into being not from out of beings and in orientation
toward them as beingness, but rather back into itself, into its truth.
The clearing of being—indicated by a meditation on the still uncomprehended [*unbegriffene*] unitary essence of thought in the sense of:
I represent something as something in the light of being. The clearing as a-byss—the nothing that is not null and naught but the proper
heavyweight, beyng itself.

14. Being differentiated from beings. The questionworthiness of the
characterization of the "relation" between being and beings as difference. The approach for the overcoming of this questionworthiness:
Being in projection; but pro-jection as *Da-sein.*

15. Negativity is swallowed up in positivity only for metaphysical
thought; the nothing is the abyssal *contrast* of beyng, but *as this its essence.* Beyng itself in its singularity; the "finitude" of beyng; what is
superficial and misinterpretable about this characterization.

16. *To think* the nothing means: to inquire into the truth of beyng
and to experience the distress [*Not*] of the totality of beings. To think
the nothing is not nihilism. The essence of nihilism consists in forgetting the nothing in the lostness to the machination[4] of beings.

17. The mastery of the machination of beings shows itself most
surely in that metaphysics, as the ground of this machination, in its
consummation degrades "being" to the status of an empty nullity.
Hegel: the "nothing" as the mere indeterminacy and unmediatedness—
thoughtlessness as such. *Nietzsche:* "being," the last fumes of evaporat-
ing reality.

3. Becoming

1. As *im-permanence*—denial of permanence. But thus ambivalent:
(a) lack of permanence—mere flow and elapsing. (b) The continual
passing-over. (c) Restlessness as *permanency* (!) of origins.

2. *Coming-to-itself*—absolute knowing as becoming (freedom!). Since
becoming (the negative [*Negative*] of the immediate) is knowledge and
actuality is thoughtness, becoming must *become* the object of thinking,
and only in thinking-itself can it "be." However, in order to think itself *un*-conditionally as a self, it must divest [*entäußern*] itself of itself
to the utmost degree (i.e., to mere being). This self-externalization

---

4. (En-framing! [*Ge-stell*!]) {later marginal note in the transcript by F. H.}

[*Selbstentäußerung*] only in order to gain itself properly and solely, and in order to *have* itself *in* the gaining, and to "be" in the having, i.e., to "be effective" in accordance with its essence. The first thing ("what") that becomes is *becoming* itself.[1] Becoming is the undetermined immediacy of coming-to-itself.

3. "Being" as immutability; ancient; Christian: Augustine, *De sermone Domini in monte* II, 7, 27;[1] *De trinitate* V, 2,3,I,6f.;[2] *De moribus Eccles. Cath.* II, 1,1.[3]

4. Negativity and the "nothing"[1]

1. The "*totally* abstract," *conceptless* ("thought"-less, the formal) *notbeing* (beginning of the *Logic*). What is *totally* abstract, i.e., still abstracted even from the *first abstraction*, the immediate, undetermined representation whose represented object still posited in its representedness and thus *negated* by the "*un-*," is the pure "nothing."

2. Abstract negativity: (a) first negation (conditioned), (b) "the second" negation—getting caught alternately in the subject-object-relationship. The "first one" already differentiates the subject and object from each other and is in *every* respect conditioned.

3. Concrete negativity—*unconditioned* negativity. The negation of "negation" as (a and b).

"Nothing"—as the not of beings. "Nothing"—as the not of being. *Negativity* must, so it seems, be encounterable in its *purest* and *most definitive* form in the "nothing"; this is indeed so, only the question remains how the "nothing" is to be comprehended here.

---

1. Saint Augustine, *De sermone Domini in monte. Patrologiae Cursus Completus: Series Latina*, vol. 34, ed. J. P. Migne (Paris, 1861). Book II, Chapter VII, 27. [English: *Nicene and Post-Nicene Fathers*, First Series, vol. 6: *Saint Augustin: Sermon on the Mount, Harmony of the Gospels, Homilies on the Gospels*, ed. Philip Schaff (Peabody, Mass.: Hendrickson Publishers, 1995).]

2. Saint Augustine, *De trinitate. Patrologiae Cursus Completus: Series Latina*, vol. 42, ed. J. P. Migne (Paris, 1861). Book I, Chapter VIf. and Book V, Chapter II, 3. [English: *Nicene and Post-Nicene Fathers*, First Series, vol. 3: *Saint Augustin: On the Holy Trinity, Doctrinal Treatises, Moral Treatises*. Edited by Philip Schaff. (Peabody, Mass.: Hendrickson Publishers, 1995).]

3. Saint Augustine, *De moribus Ecclesiae Catholicae et de moribus Manichaeorum. Patrologiae Cursus Completus: Series Latina*, vol. 32, ed. J. P. Migne (Paris, 1861). Book II, Chapter I, 1. [English: *Nicene and Post-Nicene Fathers*, First Series, vol. 4: *Saint Augustin: The Writings against the Manichaens, and against the Donatists*, ed. Philip Schaff (Peabody, Mass.: Hendrickson Publishers, 1995).]

1. Cf. Hegel's concept of being {See below section 8, and sections 15, 16, and 18.}

Hegel's "nothing": the first true thing, i.e., the first "being" in the broader sense, is becoming; it is the difference of being and nothing as the difference that is none. The nothing is not distinct from being and is not an other to it, but rather *the same.* For what reason, to what extent? Due to the interpretation of being. Since the nothing is not *something differentiated,* yet negation is "difference," negativity cannot be illuminated with the help of "the nothing." But perhaps with *being*? This, however, *the same,* therefore the other way around: i.e., *from negativity* being, which is the same as the nothing. *And thereby* perhaps the "essence" of *negativity* comes to light.

5. Negativity and being-other [Anderssein]

Something and other: Thus something becomes the one of the other and the other becomes the other of the one. The *difference* is conditioned for each side *one-sidedly.*

Only when the one becomes the other to the other of the other— when one becomes the other—, *the differences* are no longer opposed in a one-sided manner and at the same time degraded; instead they are alternately raised into the alternate belonging-together which is their *"ground"*; they lose the possibility of *conditioning* and *become themselves what is conditioned.*

Unconditioned negativity is that which is conditioned neither through the one nor through the other of the one, nor through the other of the other, but is rather detached from both and first *binds* them in their interrelation.

The three or four negations: consciousness—self—absolute knowledge.

Absolute negativity: 1. The *elevation* of the first and abstract negativity *or* its ground? 2. *If ground*—then *from where*?

Why derive absolute negativity from *one and another* (being-other), and not simply from *"nothing,"* although clearly the not-like and the *negative* appear as it were *in persona*?

6. Negativity and otherness [Andersheit]

The first negation—abstract negation. Absolute negation—the negation of negation.

Otherness—here as the essence of the other in the other itself. This is not the otherness of the other as differentiated *from the one.* This difference posits each away from the other. The other in the other itself is the *other to the other,* namely in such a way that this belongs to it as its ground but is nonetheless differentiated from it. The other of the other comports *itself to itself* in the difference.

Absolute otherness—the unconditioned relating-itself-to-itself.

7. Negativity—difference of consciousness—subject-object relationship and essence of truth

But the essence of truth? *From where and how?*

The essence of *man:* Why and to what extent to be asked as the basic question? *From where* is the essence of man to be determined? *How* is it to be determined? *Through what* is this determination itself determined (*attuned!*)? Why "attunement"?

Being-conscious [*Bewußt-sein*] (as *ego cogito* of the subject-object-relationship) and *thinking* in the sense of the *ratio* and the νοῦς of the *animal rationale.*

Hegel's "negativity" precisely *not* to be understood from the nothing and its self-sameness with "being"; because no "difference" here.

The "nothing" itself—that which is *thoughtless* pure and simple and this only within unconditioned thinking (thus from *being* in its essential sense).

No difference between being and nothing—but nevertheless: being [is] *"something differentiated,"* [and is] the *"negative" of its own negations.* Of which negations?

8. Hegel's concept of being

As that which is *un-*determined and that which can*not* be mediated, or, more precisely: *in-determinateness and un-mediatedness pure and simple.* The former is "beings" and *only* beings as such; the latter denotes the *nothing*—as the beingness of that which merely is.

That which is *not* a being is "nothing." (But "is" every nothing only that which is not a being?) For Hegel a being is something that is in some way determined and mediated.

Being "is" also *not* a being and "is" *never* a being; it is therefore the un-determined and un-mediated. Being conceived of as beingness is indeterminacy and immediacy.

The nothing (as the not of beings) is here not differentiated from being; the latter is itself the nothing, so that there is no difference—namely, there is no difference already within the thoughtness that is to be thought as the beingness of being. But nevertheless there is a difference, one that is not arbitrary and that does not turn up "here," in this beginning, but rather only "shows" itself in its most external form; it is veiled in the Hegelian sense and can never come forward *as* such, because thinking does not require it in its becoming with which it begins. Nonetheless thinking *as* the thinking of thoughtness indeed requires this difference, namely the difference between beings *and* being. Unconditioned thinking leaves this "difference" behind, or it never descends to it, and yet it is dependent on it if only in the precarious manner of a renunciation—a manner that should not escape unconditioned thinking. But it must elude the latter, because otherwise in the totality of its indeterminacy it would again have to become something conditioned [*be-dingtes*] in the highest and most complete sense, conditioned by *the* "thing" [*das "Ding"*], which is: *the totality of beings.*

This renunciation of the all-grounding difference expresses itself in Hegel's claim that the distinction between being and nothing is none. But this grounding difference is what in *Being and Time* (compare lecture course summer semester 1927, conclusion) we called "ontological difference."[1] Which "negativity" is meant here? (What is the connection with the "as": *something as a being*?)

Even here, and in spite of the unconditionedness of thinking and of thoughtness, being (in the broad sense) is conceived of *with beings in mind,* as the beingness of beings. The *Logic* too is still and indeed *wants* to be: *metaphysics.*

But now the same relation that has persisted since the beginning of the history of thinking as metaphysics (in Plato) and that constitutes the proper beginning (the difference between the totality of beings and being) is, as it were, reversed; but "as it were" only because a reversal can be discovered only from modern thought, insofar as beings in their totality would be taken as "object" [*Objekt*] in general and the "subjective" (thoughtness as being) is "as it were" swallowed up by it; whereas at the end of the history of metaphysics subjectivity as the unconditioned subject-object-relationship retains everything within itself by thinking everything in its thoughtness.

---

1. Note from the German editor: The term "ontological difference" is *not* found in the first two divisions of *Being and Time,* which were the only divisions that had been published under the title *Being and Time.* In fact, the term is mentioned for the first time in the Marburg lecture course of the summer semester of 1927, titled *Die Grundprobleme der Phänomenologie* (GA 24, p.322ff.) [English: *The Basic Problems of Phenomenology,* trans. Albert Hofstadter (Bloomington: Indiana University Press, 1982), 227ff.] In a note (p.1 [1]), Heidegger refers to this lecture course as the "new elaboration" of division 3 of part 1 of *Being and Time.*

In a historical sense, being itself is in the beginning *the being that is most in being* [*das Seiendste*] according to the mode of the totality of beings—φύσις; and in the end, the totality of beings would be dissolved into pure being as the thoughtness of unconditioned thinking, and every look back to a "being" will be thought of as decline.

9. Hegel's absolute negativity interrogated directly about its "origin"

Is this question decidable? Is it even a question? Is not Hegel's *negativity* without question one of thinking and thoughtness? "Thinking" and the "not"?

Consciousness—difference—subject-object-relationship—thinking; "I think something," and this in a transcendental sense, i.e., "as."

Thinking as the thinking of being (the beingness of beings).

Thinking (in modern thought) is both consciousness *and* difference. But in what sense? What does the coinciding of *consciousness* and difference mean?

Thinking:

1. *The thinking* of being (νοεῖν)—as fore-thinking into the supplement of the beingness of beings ("as");

2. *To consider beings* (διανοεῖσθαι)—that which asserts, judgment ("as").

How are 2. and 1. related to each other? Is 1. only a generalization of 2.?

The essence of "thinking" in the first beginning.

10. Hegel's negativity

If negativity proper—namely absolute negativity—is not merely an augmentation and an elevation of an abstract negativity into another negativity, but is rather the essential negativity as the "energy" of what is absolutely actual, then abstract negativity must conversely "arise" from unconditioned negativity. But from where does the latter arise? Admittedly, there could be no *whence* that would lie outside of absolute knowing; it is therefore all the more necessary that we inquire into the *whence* within the absolute idea. For it is still undecided what comes first within the absolute idea: *"consciousness"* (simply stated) as *I represent something—*or the *"differentiation"* that characterizes this relation of representation as *difference.*

Assuming, however, that consciousness and difference are co-originary, we must then ask in what way they are co-originary and how negation is to be grasped originarily: as the *"opposite-to,"* from which the "not" can be lifted off as "something formal,"—or as *formal differentiation,* which alone makes possible the relation of opposition.

Negativity is essentially and decisively pervasive, and it "is" unquestionably *with* the absolute idea itself, and yet the origin of negativity remains in the dark.

Or have *consciousness and difference* already become fully equated for Hegel? What would this mean?

"Consciousness"—as subject-object-relationship (difference as the self-differentiation of the subject from the object). Representation of something *as* something. The "as" in the sense of a *difference.* What kind of difference is it?

Projection upon being! Projection and *differentiation.*

The question concerning the *origin* of the *formal* "not" and "no" and concerning its *rank* surfaces everywhere. *Kant?*

The *formal* "not" *and the no; the no and the negation.* Which saying— judging—thinking? Does the not arise [*ent-springt*] from thinking? And what is the latter? Or does "thinking" grasp only the *"not"*?

Where is the origin of *negativity*? Where can it be grasped *in the purest form*? In the beginning? In *being and nothing*? But that is not a *difference.* Certainly not; being is here not the one that would be related to the nothing as the other, but being is the most unconditioned and the pure other of absolute actuality. Therefore being itself is the *most unconditioned differentiation;* not from the "nothing" but from absolute actuality.

1. It is grounded in the complete negation (that means?) of absolute negation; the contrast to all determination and mediation. So, *from where* this *complete negation* of absolute negation? *What does it mean? The complete expulsion from becoming* [*Ent-werden*] of *that which can be and has been expelled from becoming* unconditionally.

2. Furthermore, along with being and absolute actuality *being in the wider sense* (categories) is also and already *differentiated from beings.*[1] Being arises at the same time from the *complete negation* of absolute negativity and the equally *complete difference* [*Differenz*] from beings in general. *Whence these negations?* Why for instance *from* absolute negativity and with absolute *negativity*?

Being:

1. from the *dismantling* (negation) of absolute negativity; the latter is *suspended* (the un- of all determination and mediation, i.e., of all differentiation);

2. absolute actuality, whose energy is absolute negativity, itself from the *renunciation* of beings; more precisely: the renunciation of the difference between being and beings.

---

1. Compare Hegel's concept of being {See above, section 8, p.15ff.}

Dis-mantling and renunciation—what are they in light of Hegel's *meta-physics*? Is the reference to the latter a *mere idea*? Or is it the inner pos-iting of the system (not the refutation) into and through that which itself "properly" is?

* * *

Negativity as tearing and division is "death"—*the absolute lord;*[2] and the *"life* of absolute spirit" means nothing else than *suffering* and *deal-ing with death.* (But this "death" can never become a serious threat; no καταστροφή is possible, nor is any downfall and subversion [*Sturz und Umsturz*]; everything is contained and compensated. Everything is *al-ready unconditionally* secured and accommodated).

Philosophy as *ab*-solute, as *un*-conditioned philosophy must *enclose negativity* in a peculiar manner, and that basically means *not* to take it *seriously.* The *de-tachment* as *retention,* the complete conciliation in everything. There is no nothing. And that appears to be quite all right. The nothing "is" nothing and *is* not.

Dis-mantling and renunciation are the *"beginning"* of the *absolute.* Is the latter itself in its own manner the master of *these* "negations"? And how so? Or are they that which the absolute *suppresses* [*unterschlägt*] and perhaps also can suppress for *itself.*

What is their *essence?* How do they belong together?

Dis-mantling—the utmost differentiation of absolute becoming from the *expulsion from becoming* [*Ent-werden*] and *that which has been expelled from becoming.*

Re-nunciation—(the transcendental and its sublation) both are al-ready unconcerned about the essential "distinction" of *"beings and be-ing."* Is it indeed a "distinction"—or can this only count as a fore-name, as a naming that is superficial and that also covers up?

Re-nunciation—not of beings, but rather of the "difference."

Each time the question of the *thinking of being* surfaces; whether taken simply for itself and from itself, it fulfills the enactment of its possibilities, of its own essence.

The other path of the meditation on *"thinking."*

11. Review

1. The *question* concerning the "origin" of "negativity" in Hegel, i.e., in Western metaphysics as such. The question concerning Hegel: either an extraneous workaround (formal logic, the characterization of abso-lute thinking in its threefold character through "differentiatedness"—

---

2. G. W. F. Hegel, *Phänomenologie des Geistes*, ed. J. Hoffmeister (Leipzig, 1937), 148. [*Phenomenology*, §194.]

formal) *or* from consciousness. But how? That means, in its totality *every time* from *"thinking."* The *vastness and emptiness of this realm of inquiry* and its *respective* indication of the basic position. Cf. Kant on the nothing.[1]

2. *Thinking* and metaphysics. The beingness of beings and thinking. Thinking—what metaphysics makes use of as its "guiding thread"—nothing outside of it. The approach from here, no *in*trusion.

3. Thinking—judgment (is, being)—negation. Hegel's concept of judgment: the division of the "concept," i.e., of the opposites, into the opposites themselves and the combination (con-cretion [*Kon-Kretion*]) into their "unity"—the speculative "is"! To what extent nothing can be expected from the reference to the "judgment" for the illumination of the origin of negativity.

4. Being and beings as the *actual*—"actuality" and *"idea"*—*actualitas*.

5. Being and time.

12. Negativity

Hegel posits the "difference" (ἀνάλυσις/σύνθεσις) as negativity; or the other way around?

But *difference* is the *self*-differentiation of the I from the object. To be more precise, this self-differentiation is only one—the most proximal, immediate—in addition to and away from . . .

The *difference* is the essential *threefold self-differentiation* of absolute knowledge, i.e., the relating-itself-*to-itself* as the inclusion of that which is differentiated.

This *difference* is absolute *negativity* insofar as it precisely *affirms* that which is differentiated as the other in its belongingness to the one and thereby makes the one itself into the other. The *not* of the proper, i.e., unconditionally re-presenting appropriation of what is knowable in its consummate knowability of the unconditioned knowing itself *as a self.*

Thus *the fundamental question* surfaces:

1. Is *negativity* in the sense of the not-like here only *a formal workaround for the characterization* of the essential threefold differentiatedness of absolute knowledge? If yes, *from where* is negativity itself *taken* (from the "judgment" of "thinking"; and this? (A "is" B)) and with what right is it used in this way?

_____

1. Immanuel Kant, *Kritik der reinen Vernunft.* A290ff., B346ff. ("Amphibolie der Reflexionsbegriffe"). [English: *Critique of Pure Reason,* trans. Paul Guyer and Allen W. Wood (Cambridge: Cambridge University Press, 1999), 382ff. ("Amphiboly of Concepts of Reflection").]

2. Or is the differentiatedness of the *absolute* I think and of its certainty the self-evident ground of the possibility of negation? If yes, in what sense and with what right and to what extent is the "nothing" grounded thereby? (*Ground:* the whence of inner possibility.) What does the positing of I-certainty and of the *ens verum* and *certum* mean—beingness as representedness? Therein lies at once a further question:

3. How do the *not* and negativity (not-ness and the no-like)—according to 1. and to 2. respectively—relate to the *nothing* and how does the nothing relate to being? ("Yes" as approval and assent, as affirmation.)

For Hegel, negativity must apparently be understood in the sense of 2.

Separation is the "absolute power,"[1] "the innermost source of all activity";[2] the powerful is the actual, but the actual is *absolute* knowing. Knowing as knowing-itself.

But here *separation* cannot be meant only as a difference of objects—the abstract and essenceless is of that kind—, it is rather meant as *the separation* as the *essence* of *absolute consciousness*. But if the latter is that which properly is a being, then *separation—the not*—belongs to being in the essential sense (beingness). "Not" and *consciousness* are co-*originary*.

In each case, the separation of the difference brings to appearance (of representation) the lack of that which has been differentiated; but the lacking is always only the one-sided decline from the absolute self-possession of absolute knowing. Admittedly, the latter is only what it is as knowing, i.e., as the *enactment* of the movement of thought [*Denk-bewegung*].

The negative, the lack of that which is lacking, is the moving principle, not the mere *away,* but the *missing—the belonging-also-to-it.* The *negative* is therefore at bottom the self of absolute self-consciousness. The negative is the *"energy"* of *(absolute) thinking.*[3]

Separation is the "absolute" "tearing," but to the extent that it is endured and absolute spirit *preserves itself in it* (not the unmediated and non-mediating throwing-asunder). Absolute knowing is the absolute self-preservation in the tearing; this is *"life."*

Negativity is therefore at the same time *sublation.* The absolute trembling—the absolute shaking of everything. *Death* the "absolute lord."[4]

The *tarrying* of spirit *with the negative* (not the looking away) turns that which is null and naught into "being."

---

1. G. W. F. Hegel, *Wissenschaft der Logik,* ed. G. Lasson (Leipzig, 1923). Part II, Book III, 214. [*Science of Logic,* 509.]

2. Cf. ibid. Part II, Book II, 33. [*Science of Logic,* 745.]

3. G. W. F. Hegel, *Phänomenologie des Geistes.* Preface, 29. [*Phenomenology,* §32.]

4. Cf. ibid., 148. [*Phenomenology,* §194.]

13. The differentiation (separation)

The mere distinctness—one *away* from the other and only *away.* Differentiating as rejecting, dropping, passing-over.

The *difference*—where precisely the "common," the same, is held fast; and in relation to it *what is differentiated.*

The *implication*—that which is differentiated itself only as the point of departure of the *sublation* into the belonging-together.

The decision.

14. The negative

The negative for Hegel the "difference"—I *think* something—the intellect's thinking—*separation*—absolute power. The negative—the moving principle for the I and the object.[1]

The negative, i.e., *consciousness* as such—regardless of what the object of its knowing is: whether it is the object or consciousness itself as that which knows (subject) or the thought—the knowing that knows itself.

Everywhere the *negative* of the *difference* reigns from the ground up. Negation—negating—an-nihilating—wrecking—running aground.

Where is *the origin of negativity*?

How does "consciousness" acquire the determinative, all-supporting, and all-encompassing primacy?

Is negation, the differentiation, "earlier" than consciousness—or the other way around? Or both the same?

Where, then, the ground of the "not"?—I *think* something.

15. Being and the nothing

The origin [*Ur-sprung*] of the *not*—the not *in* the origin [*Ur-sprung*].

The not of beings—being (and not *the nothing*).

The not of being—the originary nothing.

The not "of" being—in the sense of a *genitivus subjectivus.* Being itself is not-like, it has in itself the nothing.

The *differentiation*—separation—presupposes the not and the nothing insofar as it *grounds* itself on the differentiability of that which

---

1. G. W. F. Hegel, *Phänomenologie des Geistes,* ed. J. Hoffmeister (1927). Preface 25ff., 29f. [*Phenomenology,* §§26ff., 32f.]

can be differentiated, which, in turn, is being (regardless of its interpretation). But is it at all possible to speak *in this manner* about Hegel and the modern interpretation of being in general (*ens = certum*)? The question is not whether this differentiation is grounded on being, but how the latter itself is comprehended and projected. But if representedness belongs to the projection of being, does not the "not" enter *being* from representation (thinking), and thus from differentiation?

But from where and how differentiation, *thinking*—the essence of *thinking*—as enactment; as the ground of the projection. Whence projection and project-openness?

Negativity and the nothing.

The nothing and the question: Why are there beings rather than nothing? The *metaphysical* character of the question, grounded in the primacy of beings.

The nothing and the essence of the ground. Ground—truth—beyng. The nothing and "*nihilism.*"

16. Hegel's concept of "being" in the narrow sense ("horizon" and "guiding thread")

Being conceived of as *indeterminacy and immediacy.* (That Hegel says: "Being is the indeterminate immediate,"[1] shows only that he equates being and beings in general understood in the ordinary sense—in accordance with the metaphysical habituation, more specifically, however, according to the idealistic mode of thinking.)

This concept of being says: The horizon of the interpretation of being is determination and mediation, more precisely determination as mediation, i.e., thinking in the sense of unconditioned thinking. Being is the thoughtness of this thinking, where being is now taken in the *broad* sense; "being" in the narrow sense is the unconditioned (or is it conditioned through and through?) *un-thoughtness* (thoughtlessness pure and simple!), thus the *complete suspension* of thinking (the non-thinking). To the extent that thinking, according to the basic position, can count only as the *representation of* "something," the suspension of thinking entails that there is *no re-presentation;* thought from the vantage point of thinking—only *only* from it—the pure void.

Hegel's concept of being thus has its *very own pre-suppositions* (namely those of the horizon of thoughtness), but these are at the same time the presuppositions of Western metaphysics; and this in turn means:

---

1. G. W. F. Hegel, *Wissenschaft der Logik*, ed. G. Lasson (Leipzig, 1923). Book I, 66, cf. also 54. [*Science of Logic*, 58; cf. also 50.]

that basic position in which the relation of Western man to beings maintains itself as such.

Therefore, Hegel's concept of being *must* at once also become understandable and reconstructable; which, according to its unconditioned basic position, must be "determined" by the "*un*" in the manner of a dismantling. In the common opinion of "beings," which has no knowledge of its horizon, it has the character of that which is simply understood and understandable (i.e., that which is projected in general), namely: of *pure presence*.

Therefore, what the meditation on Hegel's "concept" or non-concept of "being" yields is not Hegel's "standpoint" but our common Western-historical standpoint (in the bad sense of the word: a special view).

And what we call "pre-supposition" still requires an illumination of its own essence; because the designation "pre-supposition" is already somehow "proposition-like," i.e., it arises from the stance to reduce everything to *positings* and *propositions* and *thinking*, especially all first and last things. But these "presuppositions" are something different, whose essence we must comprehend and determine originarily from that *which* is allegedly only posited here.

What is that? This can only be learnt through the meditation on the essence of thinking (cf. there) and on the manner in which thinking proclaims itself the *guiding thread* and *guiding domain* of the interpretation of being; from the meditation on being and its *interpretability* and the ground of the latter, i.e., the truth of being, and the meditation on the relation of the truth of beyng to being itself.

That which holds true for Hegel's non-concept of being holds true more essentially, i.e., unconditionally, for being in the broad sense, for the absolute idea—i.e., for the having-been-sighted [*Gesichtetheit*] that sees and mirrors *itself* unconditionally; that is to say: for the presence that presences itself.

17. The "standpoint" of Hegelian philosophy is the standpoint of "absolute idealism"

Standpoint, that in which thinking stands so that what *it* has to think (being) becomes accessible for thinking, becomes *thinkable*.

Here the "standpoint" is *unconditioned thinking*; this, however, is that which is to be thought in its thoughtness itself.

The standpoint is the absolute itself; and this as the whole of "being" is what does *not require a* standpoint, and is not somehow *standpointless*. What does *not require* a standpoint, because it is through and through and everywhere the thing that *is* "accessible" to it. Everything has already reached it, and it actually only "lives" off the constant repetition of this sole present "past," of this ground-less *a priori*. The absolute—as absolute knowing—*the absolute idea*. The present that is present to itself, the presence that mirrors itself in the presencing. (Parmenides: "sphere"[1]); *unde Trismegistus dicit: 'Deus est sphaera intelligibilis, cujus centrum ubique, circumferentia vero nusquam.'*[2] No "against-which"—"beings" dissolved into beingness.

"This" absolute is unconditionally *"for itself."* Is it also unconditionally *"in itself?"* If yes—how? (Insofar as it is *only* "for itself"—re-nunciation.) If not—in what respect? Does not the *un*-conditionedness announce the most secret *condition* from which it cannot free itself; "being"; *dis*-mantling and *re*-nunciation.

The constant externalization [Entäußerung] into thoughtlessness is the *condition* of unconditioned becoming (expulsion from becoming [*Ent-werdung*] into mere being as *dis-mantling*).

The *re-nunciation* of beings, i.e., of the distinction of beings and being, is the *condition* of the unconditioned determination of being as absolute idea—*thoughtness.*

That which *conditions* here is the *complete re-nunciation* of the grounding of the difference between being and beings.

This "re-nunciation" is not expressly carried out but is made definitive only in the manner of the traditional disregard.

The pre-supposition *of thought.*

18. The (thoughtful) pre-suppositions of Hegelian thinking

Absolute thinking in its *de-tachment*—*un*-conditionedness.

1. *Dis-mantling*—of the unconditioned thoughtness, the conditionless externalization into the expulsion from becoming that makes everything that conditions disappear.

2. *Renunciation*—of the distinction between being and beings, its *interrogation* and *grounding*.

---

1. Diels-Kranz, *Die Fragmente der Vorsokratiker.* Fragment B8, Verse 43ff. Vol. I, 238. [English: Cf. G. S. Kirk, et al., *The Presocratic Philosophers: A Critical History with a Selection of Texts* (Cambridge: Cambridge University Press, 1983), 252.]

2. Thomas Aquinas, *Quaestiones disputatae de Veritate. Opera Omnia*, vol. 9 (Parma, 1859). Question II, Article III, 11. [English: *The Disputed Questions*, trans. Robert W. Mulligan, S.J. (Chicago: Henry Regnery, 1952), 68. "Hence, Trismegistus says: 'God is an intelligible sphere, whose center is everywhere, and whose circumference is nowhere.'"]

3. How, in contrast, is the *renunciation* in unconditioned thinking in Kant? *To what extent* is it *complete and definitive*? In Kant, the "ontological" difference, i.e., the distinction that is ontologically fundamental, is made explicit, but it is *not grounded* (transcendental imagination??). Hegel and absolute idealism only the beneficiaries; what do they leave out?

4. *How the dis-mantling is the essential consequence of the renunciation.* The unconditionedness of thinking points to "becoming" (as "I" think). But this in turn points to the *expulsion* from becoming [Ent-*werden*] and only *thus* Hegel's *negativity*! Thus, a highly conditioned negativity, conditioned by a more originary one.

5. Which *no and not* lie *in* this thinking itself?

6. In what respect does it "posit" the distinction between being and beings in advance?

7. Is the characterization as "distinction" appropriate here at all? "Difference"—*the carrying-apart*—yet as such it *preserves* and unfolds *the unity.* Which *unity*? How the essence of beyng?

19. The pre-suppositions of Hegelian thinking of being in the narrow and broad sense

These "pre-suppositions" as presuppositions of *thought*—*posited* with the essence of this thinking.

To posit the thinker *expressly* into the pre-supposition through this confrontation. This does not mean to go *back* to that which the thinker would have had to consider, but the transposition into that which the thinker was *not yet* allowed to and capable of considering in accordance with his essence and in accordance with his basic position; and this in order to think what he thought and precisely how he thought.

"Pre" [*Vor*]: Nothing which could or may ever be retrieved [nachgeholt] in the sense of *his* thinking, but that which is *not yet caught up to* and which is determined far in advance.

The *"limit"* of thoughtful thinking is never the *deficit* that is left behind but is the concealed undecidedness that is enforced in advance as a necessity of new decisions. In this limit lies the *greatness,* the creation of what is most inaccessible and most questionworthy, even *against* one's own knowledge. The "presuppositions" *not that which has fallen by the wayside,* but that which is thrown ahead. ("Pre-suppositions" especially not in a *"psychological-biological"* sense, but resolved upon in the essential abyss of the thinking of beyng). That which is historically essential in every thinking is the concealed encroachment into the pre-suppositions that is inaccessible to itself and therefore carried out mindlessly.[2] The grounding of that which is questionworthy can indeed never be the goal of a "world view" and of "faith," but it can be that of *philosophy,* which alone wants *being.* The *first* beginning of Western thinking carries out the broadest and richest and most concealed pre-suppositions, and its beginning consists precisely in this, not in that it supposedly starts with the least and with what is empty.

The pre-supposition, the fore-projection of that which one day is to be caught up to, is: *the groundlessness of the uninterrogated truth of beyng.*

But the catching up to this pre-supposition, the elaborating positing of the same, is not the consummation of the beginning but again a beginning and thus *more pre-supposing* than the first: beyng itself as a-byss; beings and their explicability from now on no longer the refuge, shelter, and support.

20. Review

Attempt of a *confrontation* with *Hegel,* with Western metaphysics. Confrontation—Hegel—Western metaphysics—*and positing ourselves into what is distinct and singular in each.* More could be said about this (cf. "Meditation on oneself"[1]), but before that—carry some of it out.

Focus (according to determinate demands): *negativity.*

The last time clarified through the distinction of something and other; freely taken out and dealt with. This is possible because Hegel himself knows and often says that the letter of his text is not the absolute itself. Negativity and being-other; cf. there.[2]

Negativity: the differentiatedness that differentiates itself—differentiation that is differentiated within itself—"consciousness."

"Negation" [*Negation*] always in this sense, not as "negating" [*Verneinung*] but [as] "synthesis"—elevation, but [as] determining [*Be-stimmen*].

21. The historical confrontation and the regress to "presuppositions"

"Pre-supposition"—spoken from where? "Premises," what is sent before—for calculating thinking. *First propositions* that can but do not have to be basic propositions; but even then *"propositions"? In what sense always a supplement?*

---

1. Note from the German editor: Not found in the papers on "Negativity."
2. Cf. above section 5, p.14.

The ahead[3]—how and whither and when? In what regard "simple" thinking, indeed every comportment *is ahead* of itself to the extent that it makes use of the open and openness. But what is this?

Anti-cipation [*Voraus-nahme*] and pre-possession—and the "as." Anti-cipation and pre-possession—as standing in the open. The openness of the there (there-ness). *Pre-supposing as unrecognized essential moment of Da-sein.*

But *Da-sein* not as *something present-at-hand,* merely ὑποκείμενον, that would become present-at-hand simply through a regressive inquiry, but instead: *leaping attainment* [*Er-springung*] that transforms human being [*Menschwesen*], and this one only in and from the inquiry of what is most questionworthy.

II. THE REALM OF INQUIRY OF NEGATIVITY

1. On the conceptual language

"Negativity" for Hegel: the threefold difference of immediate, mediated, unconditioned *consciousness* (*I* represent—something) that is in itself unquestioned.

"Negativity" for us the name of a *realm of inquiry:* but according to the ordinary opinion already structured in anticipation of the other inquiry, the connection of *saying-no, negation, negatedness, not, nothing, and nullity.* (How "valuative" thought, which itself is essentially bottomless, meddles even with the question of the *nothing.*)

The nothing as the a-byss, beyng itself. But here beyng not in a metaphysical sense, not in orientation toward and from beings, but from out of its truth.

However, is not the determination *a*-byss taken entirely from beings? No, it has this semblance only initially.

2. Negativity

1. Hegel's *negativity* is not a question for him; the "origin," and that means at the same time: the essential structure of that which this term comprises, does not become questionworthy and *questionable* because negativity is already posited with the "domain" of its inquiry that is presupposed by it—posited with thinking: "I represent something in general"—in its "concept," in its "thoughtness," as the thought. The only thing that matters is to think thoughtness unconditionally, and thus thinking itself.[1] Thinking therefore does not leave behind any-

---

1. Consciousness as self-consciousness and the infinity that opens up for oneself. Cf. Kant, *Welches sind die wirklichen Fortschritte, die die Metaphysik seit Leibnizens und Wolffs Zeiten in Deutschland gemacht hat?* (1791). *Akademieausgabe* XX, 270. [English: "What real progress has metaphysics made in Germany since the time of

thing that would not have been mastered in its sense, which would be undecided; unconditioned thinking is the questionlessness itself.

2. Aside from the questionlessness of *Hegel's* negativity, the *negative* is that which generally and consistently cannot at all require an interrogation; because the negative, the negated, and the negating belong to negation. Saying-no and saying-yes are originary forms of apophantic thinking. The negatedness can be "abstracted" from that which is negated as such and can be named the "*not*"; and if we apply this "not," i.e., the representing negation, to everything that can be negated—i.e., to that which is at first affirmed, the totality of beings— then we get *the nothing* as the not of the totality of beings; and this is just *nothing*—to linger here at all is already the crudest misinterpretation. Because the nothing is what is simply "*null and naught.*" It would be the annihilation, the self-annihilation of thinking if one wanted to think farther and think through that which is null and naught. The self-evidence of thinking and the fact that thinking must always have "something" to think in order to be itself entail the complete questionlessness of negativity, where "negativity" names the self-evident connection of no, negation, negatedness, not, nothing, and nullity.

3. But thinking *is self-evident,* because it guarantees the essential characteristic of man, and because man—that is us—*the thinking animal* (*animal rationale*).[2] The forms and manners of the thinking of this animal, which can always be encountered somewhere, can be described and recorded more closely, and in this process one can develop different views whose elaboration can reach varying degrees of depth. But even in its highest metaphysical system it will always remain the *retrospective* discussion of that which in its essential structure is clear and familiar. Based on this view it is therefore correct that negativity is considered to be questionless.

4. What are we driven by and to what end are we trying to tarry with what is questionless here? Is it so that we can still magically extract a question from it? Because it is precisely what is questionless that can still be ambiguous and therefore can be questionworthy.

What is questionless is on the one hand that which is not worth questioning, of which it has been definitely decided that it is unable to offer any support for an interrogation. On the other hand, that which is questionless is that which is at bottom *un*decided but which in the flight from mindfulness passes itself off as something that is decided.

Leibniz and Wolff?," trans. Peter Heath, in *Theoretical Philosophy after 1781* (Cambridge: Cambridge University Press, 2010), 362.]

2. Cf. Kant on the difference from all "beasts." Kant, *Preisschrift* on the progress of metaphysics. (See above fn.1.) Ibid. (". . . a total separation from the beasts").

The flight from mindfulness in turn can run parallel with ignorance about the decisions, but it can also already be the consequence of a willful *evasion* of decisions; indeed the two can come together in it. In this case, that which is questionless has the almost unassailable form of that which is by all means self-evident.

5. Negativity is questionless both in the system that constitutes the *consummation* of Western metaphysics and in the history of metaphysics in general. The questionlessness of negativity goes back to the questionlessness of thinking as the basic faculty of man, the positing of whose essence is itself beyond questioning. What does this questionlessness mean and what does it comprise as a whole?

Thinking "says" of a being what it *is* and how it *is*. Thinking maintains the determinative relation to the being of beings. Thinking thus also and in advance *indicates the horizon* within which being determines itself as such. Thinking is thus not only the mode of enactment of the representing determination of beings, but it is at the same time and *before* all the pregiven horizon for the essential definition of being. Being is the presence and permanence that is unconcealed for apprehension and in the apprehension. To the extent that apprehension (νοῦς) determines itself as thinking (λόγος—*ratio*, reason), being is thinkability. This determination of being *underlies in advance* both the "idealistic" and the "realistic" interpretation of the relation to beings.[3] The self-evidence of thinking therefore basically means the questionlessness of the fact that thinking is the determinative and horizon-giving relation to being.

Since thinking is the basic faculty of man, and the essence of the latter is considered to be self-evident from what was just said, the self-evidence of negativity and consequently the self-evidence of thinking means nothing less than the self-evidence *of the relationship "between" man and beyng*. From this a peculiarity arises that in various forms runs through the entire history of metaphysics: namely that man's relation to the beings that he himself is not is doubted, interrogated, interpreted, and grounded in a manifold manner, while at the same time and before all man's relation to being is beyond questioning, and this so "decidedly" that it is not even expressly considered but is asserted as the most self-evident of all that is self-evident. That which one is used to calling "ontology" is only the scholastic sealing of this self-evidence.

6. But the questionability of thinking in its essence and in its role as the pregiven horizon of the interpretation of being comprises something else that is equally questionless. Since thinking, which at first

---

3. Cf. Kant's "technology" of "nature" {Kant, *Critique of Judgment*. §23.}

immediately ponders the being that is disclosed and encountered, is at the same time the guiding thread of the determination of being, that what we call the difference between beings and being does not expressly come into view *as* a difference; and because of this every question about the essence and the ground of this difference remains altogether within the domain of what is completely indifferent and unknown.

7. What then does the metaphysical questionlessness of negativity as the questionlessness of the essence and of the role of thinking signify? That the following has remained undecided: 1. man's relation to being; 2. the difference between being and beings. These two distinctions belong together in the unity of the sole question: If the truth of being does not stem from beings, from what does being ever receive its truth and in what is this truth grounded? What is beyng if it is not a being and not the being that is most in being, but if it "is" neither a mere supplement to beings?

To inquire about negativity as the "energy" of unconditioned metaphysical thinking means to offer *this undecidedness* up to decision. To first set up this decision so that it can be seen and experienced, i.e., to make it a need, that is the sole thought of the thinking that asks the question of being. It lies in the essence of setting up this decision that, unlike any decision before, it must become a historical (not a historiological) confrontation while, at the same time, it must have carried out the leap into what is ungrounded, perhaps even into what is abyssal. Therefore, this thinking—even less so than any essential metaphysics—can never be spoon-fed in a bite-sized and doctrinal manner, as can be done with the insights of a science. What is possible, and within certain limits also necessary, is the constant and lengthy preparation for the leap into the inquiry of that which is undecided here. Such a preparation carries with it the danger of babbling about the leap instead of leaping.

3. Review

Last time we clarified once again the questionlessness of Hegelian negativity in terms of its rootedness in the common view of thinking. Most recently we have tried to view the essence of thinking in its unity and thereby to loosen up what is questionless into something questionworthy. How much we find ourselves placed in a domain of something questionworthy was shown by the fact that the question about the unitary essential ground of that which we determined to be the distinguishing mark of thinking remained without an answer and without an indication of the direction from where an answer is to be won, i.e., the direction into which we must inquire more originarily.

Perhaps we already stood at a site from which only a leap would carry us "further" and into the open, and all dissection or synopsis that seemingly takes us further only ever remains a supplement.

But for now and perhaps for a long time we act more genuinely in our thinking if we do *not* leap and instead keep the meditation in the foreground. The latter is not the foreground of a mere background (something that could be reached on the same plane) but a foreground of an *a-byss*. This barely speakable word "abyss" thinks something very sober and unique and must not be abused as an empty term that would present a merely sentimental emotion and an illusion of depth of merely rambling vague half-ideas, conceived on the spur of the moment, as serious thinking.

III. THE DIFFERENTIATION
OF BEING AND BEINGS[1]

1. Differentiation as de-cision

De-cision—here, that which *takes* out of the mere *separation* and differentiation of what can be pregiven.

Beyng itself is the *decision*—not *something that is differentiated* from beings for a representing, supervening, reifying differentiation that levels them.

Being de-cides as an e-vent in the *e-venting* of man and of the gods into the need for the essence of mankind and of divinity.—This e-venting lets the strife of the world and of the earth arise to striving,— the strife in which alone the open *clears,* in which beings fall back to themselves and receive a *weight.*

2. The differentiation of being and beings

This "differentiation," i.e., the characterization of that which is so named with the help of *difference,* is merely the foreground and is *still* metaphysical,—the outermost illumination of the ground of metaphysics within it and therefore for the common opinion always an indication and evidence and nevertheless something *misleading.*

Difference [*Unter-schied*]—carrying-apart—leap into this "not" that stems from the *nihilation that beyng is.*

The *difference* equates (cf. earlier considerations) that which is differentiated, it makes being into "something" that is ["*etwas*" *Seiendem*]. And *if not*—what does difference [*Unter-schied*] mean *then*?

---

1. Only as the superficial foreground [*vordergründig*] and the in fact pernicious determination of the relation between being and beings.

Beyng—the *"in-between" and* "beings"??

Unique—Singular
the error? of *that which always is,* i.e., *what is abandoned by being* and what is *effective* precisely in this way;

(no Platonism; no inversion of the same, no inversion of metaphysics but *an-nihilation*)

or—completely differently: *appreciation* of the refusal *as strife* of world and earth.

To differentiate:

1. *to carry apart?* or to ascertain only after the fact, namely the passage and the transition of??, *"the between"*
2. *to make equal*
3. *to abstain and look away* (mindlessly).

IV. CLEARING—ABYSS—NOTHING

1. The clearing (beyng)

Coming from "beings" and the representing comportment toward them, and seemingly analyzing these merely according to already familiar views and interpretations—we say, for instance, re-presentation is the representation of a "thing" (something) "*as*" something in the "light" of beingness (e.g., object of use—or, "animal," "living being," "equipment," "work").

This representation *of* something *as* something in the *light* of . . . is already a framework of that which in itself fits together the "of," the "as," and the "in the light of" into a unity; it is the "*clearing*" of *what is cleared* in which that which represents (i.e., man) stands, namely such that this "*standing*" in advance already determines in general the essence of man and such that it must *guide* and support this essential characterization. No longer: man and in addition and next to him this standing, but the latter and the essence of man as a question! Standing in the clearing—man is in the ground of *Da-sein.*[1] But *insistence* originarily: *mood.*

This clearing cannot be explained from beings; it is the "*between*" [*Zwischen*] *and in-between* [*Inzwischen*] (in the time-spatial sense of the originary time-space). The "of," "as," the "in the light of" are not beings, they are nothing and yet not *null and naught;* on the contrary: they are *totally* "important" [*wichtig*], of the *heaviest weight* [*Gewicht*], the proper heavyweight and the only thing in which everything that is a being (not merely as beingness, objectness, statehood) as a being "is."

The clearing is the a-byss as ground, the nihilating counterpart to all that is [*das Nichtende zu allem Seienden*] and thus *the heaviest thing.* It

---

1. Cf. *Da-sein* {see above I, section 2, p.12}.

is thus the "ground" that is never "present-at-hand" and that is never found, the "ground" that refuses itself in the nihilation as clearing—the *supporting-founding* one that *decides*, the one that e-vents—the e-vent.

The nihilation: making room for the purity of the need for grounding (refusal [*Ver-sagung*] of the ground).

The clearing: the a-byss (open to all directions) 1. of /"to"/ beings, also /to/ ourselves and those like us, 2. of the "as" that everything ultimately *is*, and that here before all *is* the *as of beyng*.

The a-byss: the *nothing*, what is most a-byssal—beyng itself; not because the latter is what is most empty and general, and what fades the most, the last fumes—but the richest, the singular, the middle that does not mediate and thus can never be taken back.

2. Being: the a-byss

It can "already" be seen with the brightest view in the experience of man from his allotment to "being."

This still as the beingness of beings, for instance in the sense of the transcendental *a priori*, and all this within the comportment of "cognition," of the "mere" representation *of* something *as* something from the view toward . . . being.

Here man (?) stands in the open *toward* something, and the latter in the free domain of the "as"; and the whole [stands] in the opening of beyng, which itself is not "object," but which "is" precisely already all this, namely this which is open, *a*-byssal and yet grounding. *The ground—as a-byss* (and at the same time refusal! [*Ver-weigerung*]). Joined together as the there and thereness in the insistence of man, an insistence that is not a property "of" man but that is the *essential* ground for him (*genitivus essentialis*).

3. Beyng and nothing

Hegel's negativity is not a negativity because it never takes seriously the not and the nihilating,—it has already sublated the not into the "yes."

The objective—states in the beingness of unconditioned thinking.

The nihilating: refusal [*Ver-sagen*] of the "ground," *a-byss*.

Beyng "is" the "nothing,"—not because each is equally as undetermined and unmediated as the other, but because they are one and yet "*fundamentally*" *different!* They are that which first opens up a "decision."

The "finitude" of being—an expression that is very misinterpretable and that at first is only a contrasting [*ab-setzender*] expression (neither "*finite*" nor infinite). What is meant is the essential connection of being and "nihilation."

4. A-byss and nothing and no

The a-byss is the ground of the *need for the nothing and of the necessity of the nihilation*, and *this* makes possible (admittedly in the long run) the *differentiation*.

The nothing the a-byss: refusal of the ground, of every support, and of every shelter in beings; but this refusal is the highest granting of the need for decision and differentiation.

The nothing is never what is "null and naught" in the sense of what is merely not present-at-hand, not effective, not valuable, non-being [*Un-seienden*], but the essential occurrence of beyng itself as that which *nihilates a-byssally*-abyssfully.

The a-byss, however, essentially as the in-between of the *need for decision* for the divine and for mankind—and thus for *Da-sein*, being-in-the-world, world and earth, strife.

Da-sein as the "*yes*" (not agreement and consent to beings) to the truth of beyng, the yes to the nihilation and to the necessity of the "no."

The "*no*" is the *yes to nihilation*. The yes to nihilation as the yes to the a-byss is the inquiry into what is most question-worthy. The guardianship of the truth of beyng is the inquirership as the acknowledgment [*Er-würdigung*] of what is most question-worthy.

But what is the distinction between being and beings? Is *this* characterization still defensible and possible as a directive for the inquiry?

5. Beyng and nothing

Whence the "*not*" and the *not*-like in all its shapes and sites? But how do we understand the "whence"? The *why*—as *for what reason* and in which manner! We mean the "ground"!

However—how do we inquire when we inquire into the *ground*? Is it *superior to that* into whose ground we are inquiring, to the "not"? Or? Do both belong together, and how?

The a-byss: *beyng. Beyng as a-byss*—*both* the nothing and the ground. The nothing is what is *a-byssally distinct from beyng as nihilation and therefore?*—*of the same essence*. The a-byss is not-like ground, not a supporting-sheltering being, and therefore of the essence of beyng.

6. "Negativity"

Beyng as the abyss is the nothing. The nothing is the extreme opposite of all that is null and naught. The *nothing* nihilates and makes possible the projection of the *not;*—the latter can be grasped as negatedness, and this, in turn, what is representable of the negation. And negation?

What is man *now*?—*Da-sein*.

What was just said is no *inversion of what was said earlier,* because being essentially something else, no longer inquired into as beingness of beings.

7. The nothing

In all metaphysics, for which being as the beingness [is] already a supplement to beings, *the nothing* is only a supplement to being. That is to say: How the nothing is determined depends in each case on how beingness is conceived. (Cf. the table of the nothing in Kant, *Critique of Pure Reason* A290ff., B346ff. [382ff.].)

V. HEGEL

1. Essential considerations concerning the conceptual language

What we call "being," in accordance with the beginning of Western philosophy, Hegel calls *"actuality"*; and this designation is not a coincidence but is pre-determined in Aristotle as the first end of this beginning: ἐνέργεια—ἐντελέχεια.

What Hegel calls "being" (and essence), and we call *"objectness"*: Hegel's designation is not a coincidence either but is determined by the *transformation of metaphysics* and by the specific character it received from Kant. Because now the being of beings (essence) as a category has the determination of *objectivity* [*Objektivität*]: *"objectness"* [*Gegenständlichkeit*].

Being and becoming. Being *as* becoming; cf. Nietzsche.

That which Hegel calls "being" is for him only a one-sided determination of *being* in *our* and (of actuality) in *his* sense.

But why [is] that which properly is the actual (the *possible* and the *necessary*)? Because—Greek—in it the full presencing of what is present, the *consummate presence*.

The re-interpretation of the "actual" (of ἐντελέχεια into *"actus"*): *what is effective,* successes.

If Hegel thus brings together the "nothing" with "being" in *his* sense, he seems to grasp the nothing only "abstractly" in a one-sided manner, and not and not even as *the nothing of actuality.* Or does he? Since being itself is nothing else than the *nothing of actuality,* the nothing is in the absolute sense the same as "being"—and it denotes that for "actuality" (beyng).

* * *

Being in our manner of speaking (*Being and Time*):

1. Beingness (ὄν ᾗ ὄν), and this in its entire history up until Hegel's "actuality" and Nietzsche's "will to power" ("life").

2. Beyng—as the ground and the permission of beingness, the original φύσις.

3. Used only for (1.). (Being and beyng.)

Accordingly the question of being: 1. as the question of beingness, 2. as the question of the truth of beyng.

"*Being*" for Hegel: Beingness in the sense of the immediate representation of the object in its objectness as re-presentedness. *Objectness.*

"Being" for Nietzsche differentiated from "becoming"; also [for] Hegel!?

2. Hegel

1. Thesis—antithesis—syn-thesis: judgment—I connect.

2. Consciousness—self-consciousness—reason (*objectivity;* "the categorial"—objectness); unity and beingness—*there.*

3. Immediacy—*mediation*—"sublation"; (connection?) linkage of 1. and 2. (*Descartes*) and *absoluteness.*

Origin of the "not" from the "absolute," the latter as "consciousness" (thinking). Unity as the gathering into the present of what is most abiding.

Thinking as the unconditioned correlation of subject and object. Categories both objective *and* subjective.

The contemplation of history—"threefold": 1. Absolute thought. 2. *Being-with-oneself as freedom; knowing* what the absolute thought is and presenting itself as it. 3. "*Being*" (*as freedom*) is "*knowing*"—unconditioned knowing (not "knowing" as belonging to being!).

Absolute concept = freedom.

Being-*conscious* / Da-*sein.*

3. "Becoming"

"*Becoming*"—(i.e., something becomes what it "is"—it goes back into itself, back into its ground = to go to the ground[4]) *to come to itself, to its essence; determining mediation.*

Hegel begins with the becoming of that which becomes, i.e., of the absolute; within this beginning he begins with "*being,*" which as *beingness* is the *nothing* of *beings,* i.e., of what is absolutely actual and its actuality.

Beginning [*Anfang*]—*from which* something emerges [*ausgeht*] as that in which it remains and into which it grounds itself in emerging.

Inception [*Beginn*]—with which the emergence starts [*anhebt*] and what disappears as such, that from which one moves on and which is put away, that which is surmounted and that means at the same time is sublated.

Hegel begins with the *beginning,* this beginning is the absolute conception of the *ego cogito*—a properly modern interpretation of the ἐν ἀρχῇ ἦν ὁ λόγος.[5] "Being" (actuality) as being-conscious, i.e., to be conscious of something, of an object, to have the latter for oneself as an object-of-consciousness.[6]

4. The pure thinking of thinking

The *pure thinking of thinking* and of *that which it thinks* in *immediacy*. That and how thinking as the guiding thread and the ground of the projection of the truth of being.

This a thinking from out of *absolute thinking*. (Cf. being and becoming, being and negativity, being and reason.)

5. "The higher standpoint"

"*The higher standpoint* which the self-consciousness of spirit . . . has achieved with respect to itself, . . ."[1] (since the *Critique of Pure Reason*, through Fichte, Schelling, Hegel's *Phenomenology of Spirit*). To know *itself as such*—self-consciousness as the knowledge of the consciousness of the object. "Self-knowledge" the "basic determination" of the "actuality" of spirit.

The former metaphysics transformed. *Metaphysics* now: the "pre-occupation" of (absolute) spirit "with its pure essence."[2] "The substantial form of spirit has reconstituted itself."[3] What used to be *metaphysica generalis* now becomes "*metaphysics proper*"[4] (or, the peak of metaphysics proper becomes the absolute *metaphysica generalis*), because in the *Science of Logic* absolute spirit, "god," is purely with himself. Theology was formerly the highest stage of metaphysics proper and the *metaphysica generalis* was only an empty vestibule.

"The impatience of incidental reflection."[5] When the mere idea is *not* an *in*trusion—, when the whole as such is tackled in its unquestioned and unquestionable ground.[7]

Until the consummation of German Idealism, philosophy still remains supported and sheltered by the questionlessness of its basic position (certainty) and by the general aim and the interpretation of the totality of beings (Christianness). Since then a transformation has been in the making—unsupported and unsheltered,—even though

---

1. G. W. F. Hegel, *Wissenschaft der Logik*, ed. G. Lasson (Leipzig, 1923). Preface to the first edition, 3. [*Science of Logic*, 7.]

2. Cf. ibid. [*Science of Logic*, 7.]

3. Ibid., 5. [*Science of Logic*, 8.]

4. Ibid. [*Science of Logic*, 8.]

5. Ibid. Preface to the second edition, 21. [*Science of Logic*, 21.]

for the time being and despite multiple modifications everything still remains what it used to be. Another historicity of thinking begins; the first thinker, who still is a transitional thinker, is Nietzsche. Between them scholarliness, historicism.

6. Hegel's "impact"

Hegel and German Idealism in general have remained without impact in terms of their proper system,—because not comprehended and because it posits itself as the consummation; thus only a historical oddity which so-called "life" has never bothered and will never bother to comprehend. Without "impact."

But what does "impact" mean? How does a philosophy "have an impact"? Is it even essential to have an impact?

1. An impact by *triggering opposition,* i.e., the negation of philosophy, invoking the opposite: Thus also Schopenhauer—"life"—Nietzsche. Fact, progress, the tangible, that which confirms *immediately.*

2. That in this process concepts and conceptions are adopted and modified, only a consequence.

3. That a school and "philology" and scholarliness of the philosophy in question is produced is a matter of indifference. "Hegelianism" and the like.

The unusual fruitfulness of Hegel's standpoint and principle and at the same time the complete boringness of the same;—that nothing further happens and that nothing further can happen.

Hegel is right when he declares "beings" and the actual of the immediate (true-to-life) representation and production to be the "abstract" (what is *one-sided,* abstracted, untrue). But what for him is *comprehensive,* what is brought along, what is true is "only" the (seemingly) unconditioned justification of the abstract—the most abstract, because the truth of beyng is that which is utterly unquestioned and unquestionable.

Where is the origin of Hegel's "negativity"? Does Hegel *show* this origin, and how? "Negativity" and "thinking" as the guiding thread of the metaphysical interpretation of being. The μὴ ὄν[1]—"privation"— the opposition—the not.

---

1. {Hand-written supplement from the 1941 revision:} Plato's μὴ ὄν; to what extent was negativity seen and how is this sight connected to the ἰδέα. *The "discovery" of the privative–of the* μὴ ὄν *as* ὄν. Historically: Heraclitus *and* "Parmenides."

If Plato recognizes that-which-is-not as a being [*das Nicht-seiende als Seiendes*] and thus determines being in richer terms, the decisive question still remains, namely how he conceives of being—everything ἰδέα; whether, despite the whole recognition of the privative, being *and* even more so the "negative" are not misrecognized.

The fullness and wholeness of the absolute as the condition of *what is one-sided.* Whence the one-sidedness? One-sidedness and *"subjectivity."* Subjectivity and thinking. In what way is subjectivity many-sided? The "sides" (directions) of re-presentation (thing, I, I-thing-*relation* itself; why not into infinity?).

7. Metaphysics

Being as beingness (re-presentedness).

Beingness as being-asserted (the categorial); cf. being—captured in the predicate (the categorial).

The categories—both "objective" and "subjective"—as "objective" or "subjective"—absolute.

The "subjective" as the thoughtness of the finite ego or of *absolute* (subjective-objective) *spirit.*

The *thoughtness* as such of "thinking" in the service "of *life"* (Nietzsche).

Thinking as form of enactment—thinking as guiding thread; cf. *Being and Time.* The unity of the two.

The first beginning and its end. Hegel—Nietzsche.

8. On Hegel

1. Not some *"still* higher standpoint" than Hegel, i.e., one of spirit and thus of modern metaphysics.

2. No such standpoint of spirit at all but one of *Da-sein,* and that means:

3. No metaphysical standpoint at all or beingness of beings, but of beyng; "metaphysics" in the broadest and at the same time proper sense.

4. If this a "standpoint" at all,—rather a transition as (standing forth [*Er-stehen*]) going toward (event).

The confrontation must never become a merely "incidental reflection";[1] that means, the standpoint, conceived as a basic metaphysical position, must be pursued from the ground of its own inquiry, and that means the basic position as a metaphysical basic position must at the same time be taken back from the guiding question (unfolding in the "system of science"[2]) into the basic question.

---

1. G. W. F. Hegel, *Wissenschaft der Logik,* ed. G. Lasson (Leipzig, 1923). Preface to the second edition, 21. [*Science of Logic,* 21.]

2. Ibid. Preface to the first edition, 7. [*Science of Logic,* 11.]

9. *"The logical beginning" ("pure being")*

This beginning "is to be made in the element of a free, self-contained thought, in pure knowing."[1] Pure knowing—*immediacy.* "Pure knowing" is "the ultimate and absolute truth of consciousness"[2]—pure knowing *as* "consciousness" (and as truth)—*mediation.*

Hegel begins *"with"* "absolute knowing" (*even* in the *Phenomenology of Spirit*). What does beginning (of thinking) mean here? Not inception—where to proceed means to go forward—but that *to which* thinking holds on, *that wherein thinking has contained itself in advance.* But why is this containing necessary.

Pure knowing—"a certainty that has become truth."[3] Certainty: the knowing-oneself as knowledge, being *oneself* the object and objectness. "Knowledge" as it were vanished—"pure being";[4] the having-withdrawn[5] as such. Truth here taken in the transcendental sense!

Pure knowing has *divested* itself from everything that is "other," that could not be it itself, i.e., there is no other, no difference to the other—"the distinctionless."[6] *"What is empty"*[7] is therefore simply the beginning of philosophy.

To what extent is it in the nature of the beginning (of thinking) (*as the thinking of thinking*) that it is *being*?

Beginning and consummation—unconditionedness of thinking.

---

1. G. W. F. Hegel, *Wissenschaft der Logik,* ed. G. Lasson (Leipzig, 1923). Book I, 53. [*Science of Logic,* 46.]
2. Ibid. [*Science of Logic,* 46.]
3. Ibid. [*Science of Logic,* 47.]
4. Ibid., 54. [*Science of Logic,* 47.]
5. Ibid. [*Science of Logic,* 47.]
6. Ibid. [*Science of Logic,* 47.]
7. Ibid., 66. [*Science of Logic,* 55.]

APPENDIX

Supplement to the title page

{Editor's note: The following references are handwritten notes by Heidegger on the title page of the transcript by Fritz Heidegger; cf. afterword of the German editor.}

—Cf. *Mindfulness* typescript p.431ff.[1]
—Cf. *Metaphysics as History of Being.*[2]
—Cf. *Overcoming Metaphysics* and continuation I.[3]
—Cf. *History of Beyng* and continuation.[4]

Supplement to I, section 1 (p.3)

Not to disrupt or distract the exercises—in their own course—, nor to force one's way to Hegel's philosophy from the outside by means of an inquiry, but from its own standpoint and its "principle."

If there a necessity and need, if Hegel still something that is "actual" [*Wirkliches*], if Hegel [has] ever been something with an impact [*Wirksames*]. "Beside the point"—every "philosophy."

---

1. Unpublished treatise from division III of the *Gesamtausgabe*. [Published in 1997 as *Besinnung* (GA65). English translation by Parvis Emad and Thomas Kalary as *Mindfulness (Besinnung)* (New York: Continuum, 2006).]

2. Martin Heidegger, *Nietzsche II*, 399–454. Verlag Günter Neske, Pfullingen 1961. [English translation in: *The End of Philosophy*, trans. Joan Stambaugh (New York: Harper & Row, 1973).]

3. Unpublished treatise from division III of the *Gesamtausgabe*. [Published in 2000 as part of *Vorträge und Aufsätze* (GA7). English translation in *The End of Philosophy*.]

4. Unpublished treatise from division III of the *Gesamtausgabe*. [Published in 1998 as part of *Die Geschichte des Seyns* (GA69).]

Which "standpoint" of thinking? *Absolute* idealism; against the philosophy of reflection and according to the "principle." How [is this] philosophy determined? Which principle?

Ground of the system: Substance is subject;[1] "being" is "becoming," yet according to the standpoint its beginning. Preface: Substantiality is subjectivity (the *I* think); being is becoming—beingness and thinking.

How do we proceed to the exposition of "negativity"? (Cf. "Introduction" and *"Preface"* to the *Phenomenology of Spirit*). Substance as subject.

Thinking as a form of enactment; the pregiven guiding thread of the interpretation. Thinking [is] the guiding thread; beingness—thoughtness; but thinking [is] asserting (cf. *Being and Time*).

---

1. G. W. F. Hegel, *Phänomenologie des Geistes*, ed. J. Hoffmeister (Leipzig, 1937). Preface, 20. [*Phenomenology*, §17.]

ELUCIDATION OF THE "INTRODUCTION" TO HEGEL'S "PHENOMENOLOGY OF SPIRIT"

(1942)

PRELIMINARY CONSIDERATION

On the varied role and position of the "Phenomenology
of Spirit" within Hegel's metaphysics

The work that we call, in short, Hegel's *Phenomenology of Spirit* was published in 1807 under the full title: *System of Science. Part One. The Phenomenology of Spirit.* The proper body of the work begins with a deliberation that in its next publication in the complete edition of his works[1] comprised nearly thirteen pages and carried the explicit title "Introduction" (WW II, 59–72 [§§73–89]).[2] With certain reservations we may call this deliberation "Introduction" even though this title is missing from the first edition. Already in the first edition the "Introduction" is preceded by an extensive "Preface" (WW II, 3–58 [§§1–72]) that in this edition comprises forty-one pages. In some copies of the first edition,[3] a title page for the *entire* work can be found *after* the preface and *before* the "Introduction," bearing the heading "Science of the Experience of Consciousness." During the printing Hegel replaced this title with the following one: *Science of the Phenomenology of Spirit.* In the complete edition of his works, which was commenced and attended to by Hegel's students immediately after Hegel's death, this work appeared in 1832 under the title *Phenomenology of Spirit.* (Hegel himself had already used this title in the introduction to the *Logic* 1812 p.X. [28])[4] The determinate and determining article "the" is omitted.

---

1. G. W. F. Hegel, *Werke: Vollständige Ausgabe durch einen Verein von Freunden des Verewigten.* 19 vols. (Berlin 1832–45 and 1887).

2. Ibid., vol. II, *Phänomenologie des Geistes,* ed. Johannes Schulze (Berlin, 1832, second edition 1845).

3. G. W. F. Hegel, *System der Wissenschaft: Erster Theil, die Phänomenologie des Geistes,* (Bamberg and Würzburg: Joseph Anton Goebhardt, 1807).

4. G. W. F. Hegel, *Wissenschaft der Logik,* 2 volumes (Nürnberg: Johann Leonhard Schrag, 1812–13 and 1816).

Shortly before his death Hegel had begun to revise this work; so it may be assumed that this change of the title and also the insertion of the heading "Introduction" stem from Hegel himself.

The title was changed for a weighty reason. The *Phenomenology of Spirit* had to forfeit its "role" as "Part One" of the system because the *System* itself had in the meantime changed in Hegel's thinking. According to the advertisement that was written *by Hegel* himself and that appeared in the *Jena Allgemeine Literatur-Zeitung* on October 28th, 1807, a second part was planned for *the System of Science,* whose first part was the *Science of the Phenomenology of Spirit:* "A *second volume* will contain the system of *logic* as speculative philosophy, and the remaining two parts of philosophy, the *sciences* of *nature* and of *spirit.*"[5]

Indeed five years later the announced "speculative" logic began to appear under the title *Science of Logic.* This title correlates to the title of "Part One" of the *System of Science* from 1807: *Science of the Phenomenology of Spirit.* Yet, in 1812 the *Science of Logic no* longer appeared under the overarching title *System of Science.* Nor is the *Science of Logic* edited according to Hegel's own advertisement from 1807 as the *"second* volume" or the *"second* part" of the system. In the years 1812 and 1813 the first volume of the *Logic* appeared in two books that contain the "Objective Logic"; in 1816 the second volume appeared, which concludes the work with the "Subjective Logic" or the "Doctrine of the Concept." The "Sciences of Nature and Spirit," which had also been announced in Hegel's own advertisement from 1807 for the second part of the "system," did not appear at all. We know indeed that during his teaching activity in Jena (1801–1806) Hegel repeatedly and extensively lectured on the philosophy of nature and of spirit.[6] Pieces from these lectures went into the *Phenomenology of Spirit,* albeit in a modified form. Thus the publication of the "Sciences of Nature and Spirit" was not omitted because Hegel had not worked on these areas but for another essential reason.

During the time between 1807 and 1812, the *System* whose first part consists of the *Phenomenology of Spirit* must have changed. We call

---

5. G. W. F. Hegel, *Phänomenologie des Geistes,* ed. Johannes Hoffmeister (Leipzig: Meiner, 1937). "Editor's Introduction," xxxviii.

6. G. W. F. Hegel, *Jenenser Realphilosophie (Natur- und Geistesphilosophie). II. Die Vorlesungen 1805–1806,* ed. Johannes Hoffmeister (Leipzig: Meiner, 1931).

[English: *Hegel and the Human Spirit: A Translation of the Jena Lectures on the Philosophy of Spirit (1805–06) with Commentary,* trans. Leo Rauch (Detroit: Wayne University Press, 1983).

The Jena System, 1804–5: Logic and Metaphysics, trans. John W. Burbridge and George di Giovanni (Kingston: McGill-Queen's University Press, 1986).]

the system that was determined by the *Phenomenology of Spirit* by the short name "Phenomenology-system." One year after the completion of the *Logic,* which appeared between 1812 and 1816 without any explicit assignment into a system as its own part of the system, in 1817 Hegel published a work titled *Encyclopaedia of the Philosophical Science in Outline, for Use in His Lectures.*[7]

Hegel began his teaching in Heidelberg in the winter semester of 1816–17 with a lecture on the *Encyclopaedia.* The almost simultaneous *publication* of the *Encyclopaedia* had its "most immediate occasion" in the "need to supply my listeners with a compendium."[8] But the *inner* reason of the publication is the change of the system into *the* shape that Hegel considered to be the *definitive* one and that he retained *as* such. He therefore says in the preface to the *Encyclopaedia:* "In an 'outline,' where the content is one that is already presupposed and familiar and that is to be presented with deliberate concision, what comes into consideration is that the order and arrangement of the topics be *externally suitable.* Since the present exposition is not like that but sets out a new treatment of philosophy according to a method that, I hope, will eventually be recognized as the only veritable one, the one that is identical with the content, I could have considered it more beneficial for the public—if my circumstances had permitted this—to let this treatment be preceded by a more extensive work on the other parts of philosophy, like the one I have presented to the audience about the first part of the whole, the *logic.*"[9]

Certain decisive things become clear from these remarks:

1. The *Encyclopaedia* is at bottom not a textbook but rather the shape of the new and definitive system. We call it in short "Encyclopaedia-system."

2. This system now no longer takes the *Science of the Phenomenology of Spirit* as its first part but instead the *Logic.*

3. In the preface to the *Encyclopaedia* Hegel *explicitly* refers to the *Science of Logic* that he had completed in the preceding year and that thereby receives an outwardly *ambiguous* position. At first it still seemed to be the second part of the Phenomenology-system, but when it ap-

7. G. W. F. Hegel, *Encyclopädie der philosophischen Wissenschaften, Zum Gebrauch seiner Vorlesungen* (Heidelberg: August Oßwald, 1817).

8. Cf. ibid., beginning of the preface (to the first edition). WW VI, ed. Leopold v. Henning (Berlin, 1840), iii. [English: *The Encyclopaedia Logic: Part 1 of the Encyclopaedia of Philosophical Sciences with the Zusätze,* trans. T. F. Geraets et al. (Indianapolis: Hackett, 1991), 1; translation modified.]

9. Ibid. Preface. WW VI, ivf. [English: *The Encyclopaedia Logic,* 1; translation modified.]

peared it is in fact already the first and fundamental part of a new system, the Encyclopaedia-system.

4. In the preface to the *Encyclopaedia* Hegel *no longer* mentions the *Phenomenology of Spirit* because it was not only no longer the first part of the system; it was no longer a main part of the system at all.

The fact that the "Phenomenology-system" had already been given up by the time the *Logic* was published in 1812—five years after the *Phenomenology*—can be presumed from the fact that the complete title *System of Science* and its designation as "Part Two" are missing. We can gather from the *Philosophical Propaedeutic,* edited by Karl Rosenkranz in 1840 in Volume XVIII of the *Complete Works,*[10] that the Encyclopaedia-system was already established between 1808 and 1811. Moreover, the arrangement of the teaching material of the *Philosophical Propaedeutic,* which Hegel presented as a teacher at the Nuremberg Gymnasium, reveals very clearly the primacy of the Encyclopaedia-system:

First seminar. For the Lower Grade: doctrine of right, deontology, theory of religion.

Second seminar. For the Middle Grade: phenomenology of spirit and logic.

Third seminar. For the Higher Grade: doctrine of the concept and philosophical encyclopaedia.[11]

Here the proper completion of the logic appears as the beginning and foundation of the Encyclopaedia-system. Yet, in this system the phenomenology of spirit is not erased. It is incorporated into the Encyclopaedia-system in a modified function. This system has three parts:

A. The science of logic.
B. The philosophy of nature.
C. The philosophy of spirit.

The third part is again subdivided into three parts:

Part 1: Subjective spirit.
Part 2: Objective spirit.
Part 3: Absolute spirit.

---

10. G. W. F. Hegel, *Werke: Vollständige Ausgabe durch einen Verein von Freunden des Verewigten.* Vol. XVIII, *Philosophische Propädeutik,* ed. Karl Rosenkranz (Berlin, 1840). [English: *The Philosophical Propaedeutic,* trans. A. V. Miller (Oxford: Basil Blackwell, 1986).]

11. WW XXVIII, 1, 77, 121. [English: *The Philosophical Propaedeutic,* 1, 55, 105.]

Part one of the third main part of the system, the philosophy of the subjective spirit, is in turn arranged into three sections:

A. Soul.
B. Consciousness.
C. Spirit.[12]

In the introductory paragraph 307 of part one of the third main part of the system it says: "subjective spirit {is}
(a) immediate spirit, *natural spirit,*—the object of what is usually called *anthropology,* or the *soul;*
(b) spirit as the identical reflection into itself and into another, *relation* or particularization—*consciousness,* the object of the *phenomenology* of spirit;
(c) *spirit that is for itself,* or spirit as *subject;*—the object of what is ordinarily called *psychology.—Consciousness awakens* in the *soul;* consciousness *posits itself* as *reason;* and subjective reason frees itself into objectivity through its activity."[13] This threefold distinction of the subjective spirit can historically be explained by means of the distinction of *anima, animus sive mens,* and *ratio.*[8]

The *Phenomenology of Spirit* has now become the middle portion of part one of the third main part of the system. Instead of supporting and determining the systematics of the system as the first part, as it had formerly done, the *Phenomenology* now disappears into a corner of the systematics of the definitive system. In terms of its doctrinal content the *Phenomenology of Spirit* has remained the same, yet in the new system it has a very different and a very restricted systematic function.

Hegel further expanded the content of the Encyclopaedia-system in the following years. Compared to the first shape of 1817, the so-called Heidelberg *Encyclopedia,* the second edition of 1827 is considerably more extensive; the third one of 1830 has been expanded even further. In the second edition Hegel included the address he delivered to his audience on the occasion of the commencement of his professorship in Berlin on October 22, 1818. The *concluding sentence* of this address characterizes the *general orientation* of the Encyclopaedia-system and thus of Hegel's metaphysics in general: "The essence of the uni-

_____

12. WW VI, table of contents, xi–xvi. [English: *The Encyclopaedia Logic,* "Contents," 4–7.]

13. *Encyclopädie der philosophischen Wissenschaften* [1840], 209. [English: *Hegel's Philosophy of Mind,* trans. William Wallace and A. V. Miller (Oxford: Clarendon Press, 1971), §387; translation modified.]

verse that is at first concealed and closed contains no power that could withstand the courage of cognition; it must open up before it and lay its riches and its depth before its eyes and offer them for its enjoyment."[14]

The construction of the Encyclopaedia-system shows a decisive realignment with the basic structure of earlier metaphysics. The primacy of the *Science of Logic* corresponds to the *metaphysica generalis*. The philosophy of absolute spirit corresponds to the conclusion of the *metaphysica specialis* (metaphysics *proper* in the Kantian sense), i.e., of the *theologia rationalis*. The philosophy of nature corresponds to the *cosmologia rationalis* and the philosophy of subjective and objective spirit corresponds to the *psychologia rationalis*. Hegel indeed adheres to this inherited basic structure already in the Phenomenology-system, but he does so only in the second part of the system.

However, these remarks characterize the *transformation* from the Phenomenology-system to the Encyclopaedia-system only externally. The question of the *inner* necessity of this transition and of its metaphysical significance, the question of the concealed equal status and of how the two systems belong together within Hegel's metaphysics, the questions of the essence and of the unfolding of the system character that is the distinguishing mark of modern metaphysics as such: all these questions require a mindfulness that lies outside the horizon of "historiological" Hegel scholarship. The elucidation of the *Phenomenology of Spirit* that is attempted here wants to prefigure the sphere of such mindful meditations and thereby aims to suggest that this metaphysics concerns us now and in the future with the same immediacy as the oldest saying of Western thinking.

When at the end of the address mentioned above Hegel says that the "universe," which for him is the same as the absolute, has in itself no power of resistance to assert its concealed essence against the disclosing courage of metaphysical cognition, the question arises as to *why* the absolute lacks this power of resistance. The answer is: Because the absolute is, in accordance with its essential character, unable to resist this disclosure, but, on the contrary, it *wants* to reveal itself. This will to show itself is its essence. Appearance is the essential

---

14. G. W. F. Hegel, *Encyklopädie der philosophischen Wissenschaften im Grundrisse, Zum Gebrauch seiner Vorlesungen,* second edition (Heidelberg: August Oßwald, 1827).—The inaugural address mentioned here has been included in vol. XIII of the complete edition of Hegel's works published by the association of friends. Cf. ibid., vol. XIII, *Vorlesungen über die Geschichte der Philosophie,* vol. I, ed. Karl Ludwig Michelet (Berlin, 1833), 6. [English: *Political Writings,* trans. H. B. Nisbet (Cambridge: Cambridge University Press, 1999), 185; translation modified.]

will of spirit. It is with an eye toward this essential will of the absolute that Hegel's statement is made. This essential determination of the absolute is, therefore, the presupposition of the Encyclopaedia-system. But what about the presupposition itself? Can the system lay claim to being the absolute system if it rests on a presupposition that it does not ground itself, namely in an absolute sense? Hegel indeed carried out the grounding of this essence of the absolute and managed to carry it out in the *Science of the Phenomenology of Spirit. If* the absolute wills to reveal itself because it is the will to manifestation, then self-revelation, i.e., appearance, *must* belong to the essence of the absolute. Essence and appearance are identical here. The absolute is spirit. Spirit is the knowing that knows itself as the essential ground of all beings and that wills itself in this knowledge. Spirit is absolute knowledge. Since appearance belongs to its essence, absolute knowledge has to present itself as appearing knowledge. This is the only way in which absolute knowledge *itself* [*von sich aus*] grants the courage of human cognition the possibility to be open *for* this cognition and to be *with* what is cognized in this cognition in the first place. Conversely, insofar as human cognition knows the absolute, it must above all bring the self-presentation of appearing knowledge to realization. *If* this realization of the self-presentation of the appearing absolute *is to be suitable for the absolute,* then it can itself only be *absolute.* Science, in turn, must bring this absolute self-presentation to its absolute realization. If the *Phenomenology of Spirit* is this realization, then the work that bears this title has dared to undertake a metaphysical task that never before needed to be assigned and that afterward could never be assigned again. This "work" is, therefore, a unique and in a special sense distinguished moment in the history of metaphysics. By "work" we do not mean the intellectual achievement of the human being Hegel, but "work" as the happening of a history in and for the sake of which a unique constancy and determination (the insistence of *Da-sein*) is demanded from all human accomplishments.

Hegel knew in his own way of the uniqueness of the task of the *Phenomenology of Spirit,* and he made no mistake about its essential difficulty. Otherwise he would not have provided this work with a special "Introduction" and have this "Introduction" preceded by a "Preface" for which there are no comparable precedents in the history of Western thinking.

If they have a function at all, "prefaces" and "introductions" are meant to lead into the work and to provide "outsiders" with a bridge to the entrance into the work. In the "introductions" to works of the sciences this task can be performed without difficulty because everyday representation and scientific thinking remain directed straightforwardly toward beings. An "introduction" to *philosophical* thinking is impossible; for there exists *no* steady and deliberate gliding-over from everyday thinking into thoughtful thinking, because the latter deals with being and because being can never and nowhere be encountered among beings as a being. The *only* thing that exists here is the leap and the leap into it. An "introduction" can only serve as a preparation for the leap, i.e., to bring the rift between the comportment toward beings and the thinking of being that we need to leap over into the field of vision, and to not make the approach to the leap too short. (Why is this possible? The pre-philosophical understanding of being.) But every introduction "into" "philosophy" still has to come to an understanding with those who do not stand in it and has to get involved with *their* horizon of understanding. In doing this, the "introduction" acts always and necessarily against its own intention.

Nevertheless it does not have to be in vain—as a preparation for the leap into the thinking that thinks the being of beings. However, in Hegel's metaphysics—and in the metaphysics of *German Idealism* in general—we not only have to think being but it is necessary to think beings in their being *as* the absolute absolutely, in an *absolute manner*. This requires a leap that, in turn, must still leap over itself: the absolute leap into the absolute. The presentation of the *Phenomenology of Spirit* dares to accomplish this leap.

From these remarks it becomes clear that our attempt to elucidate what the *Phenomenology of Spirit* is remains in all respects thought-provoking. How are we to proceed if on top of this we presuppose neither the knowledge of the work itself nor that of the "Preface" and of the "Introduction"? We use the help that Hegel himself provided in the form of the "Introduction" to his work. By doing this, we must, however, take these few pages in advance as that which they must eventually be recognized and understood to be. For they are the explanation *of* the title that stands *before* the entire work and that is: *Science of the Experience and Consciousness.* Now, it was precisely *this* title that Hegel dropped during the printing. It remained only on a few copies of the first edition (1807). Hegel replaced the crossed-out title with the ultimate version: *Science of the Phenomenology of Spirit.* In the edition of the *Phenomenology* that is part of the collected works (1832), which is the one that is most commonly used, the crossed-out title is missing, so that the "Introduction" which refers to it is left without any explicit mention of *the* respect in which it speaks. Moreover, in comparison to the massive "Preface" the "Introduction" appears to be of minor importance, so that at most one occasionally takes this or that passage from it as a "quotation"—and they are always the same uncomprehended passages. The "Introduction" lays out *why* the *Sci-*

ence of the Experience of Consciousness is necessary and what it is from the ground of its necessity. If we juxtapose the *second* title—*Science of the Phenomenology of Spirit*—we notice immediately, albeit at first only formally, the following: The "phenomenology of spirit" is "the experience of consciousness." To elucidate the *Phenomenology of Spirit* thus means: to explain on the basis of the "Introduction" what Hegel thinks in the domain of absolute metaphysics and "speculation" when he speaks of "experience"; it means to expound how that which is called "the experience of consciousness" is to be understood; it means to expound in what sense the *Science of the Experience of Consciousness* has to be thought (cf. below p.78ff.). In order to gain clarity on this, we must first elucidate what the term "consciousness" means in modern metaphysics.

"Consciousness" is the not entirely obvious name for *conscientia,* i.e., for *that* knowledge which also knows all modes of comportment of man, insofar as these refer to the *mens,* the "spirit." "Spirit" expresses itself, i.e., itself *as a self,* by saying "I." Insofar as consciousness, as the co-knowing of the known and of its knowing, "is" the relation to the self, it *is self-consciousness.* The essence of consciousness is self-consciousness; every *cogito* is an *ego cogito me cogitare.* The *videre* and *ambulare* is also a *cogitare* provided that they are truthful, that is provided that they are certain, in the manner of the *cogitatum* in the *cogito me videre, cogito me ambulare.* Descartes, therefore, says in §9 of the first part of *Principia philosophiae* 1646: *Cogitationis nomine, intelligo illa omnia, quae/nobis consciis/in nobis fiunt, quatenus eorum in nobis conscientia est.*[15] "By the term 'thought' ('consciousness'), I understand everything we know *along ourselves,* everything that occurs in us *insofar* as there exists an accompanying-knowing of all this in us."[9]

Consciousness is not merely *perceptio,* a grasping placing-before [*Vorstellen*], but *apperceptio,* a placing-toward-*ourselves* that grasps *us* also. But according to its essence, the self that is thus represented alongside does not move into consciousness after the fact and in addition to that which consciousness is also conscious of, while consciousness otherwise remains immediately directed toward the things. Self-consciousness is not a consciousness that has been *enriched* in its content with the representation of the self; rather, the consciousness of things is *essentially* and *properly self-*consciousness, albeit one that most of the time does not

---

15. Descartes, *Principia philosophiae.* §9. *Œuvres de Descartes,* ed. Charles Adam and Paul Tannery (Paris, 1897–1910). Vol. VIII, 1, p.7. [English: *Principles of Philosophy,* trans. Valentine Rodger Miller and Reese P. Miller (Dordrecht: D. Reidel Publishing, 1983), 5. "By the word 'thought,' I understand all those things that occur in us while we are conscious, insofar as the consciousness of them is in us."]

represent the self distinctly [*eigens*] and thus in a sense forgets about it. The self in self-consciousness is *both* one *side* of the relation of consciousness to the object-of-consciousness and *at the same time*, and that means *properly*, the entire relation itself. This relation contains the basic constitution of consciousness. Hegel calls it "reflection," though he does not take this term psychologically as a comportment but rather ontologically as the structural relation of the essential bending and of the shining back of every object-of-consciousness as such, and thus of consciousness, into the self. Hegel understands "reflection" not as a turning back of the *gaze* but as the bending back of the shining and the appearance, i.e., of *light* itself. ("Reflection" is taken in a metaphysical ontological sense, not a subjective-psychological sense; cf. already Kant in the "Amphiboly of Concepts of Reflection"). (The essential unity of "reflection" and negativity; consciousness is spirit as the identical reflection into itself and into another.)

Since consciousness is essentially self-consciousness and must be comprehended from the self, yet the self steps *out* of itself *toward* the object and shows itself and appears during this process, consciousness as self-consciousness is the *appearing* knowledge. Consciousness is essentially the *element* and the *ether of the appearance* of knowledge, which itself *is* only as self-knowledge, i.e., as *mens sive animus*, i.e., as spirit.

That the human being is a self and is able to say "I" and knows of itself and has "self-consciousness" has always been known by Western thinking. Heraclitus says (Fragment 101): ἐδιζησάμην ἐμεωυτόν.[16] "I have—pursuing my self—listened into it." But these "conversations" of the soul "with itself" of the Greeks and in Christianity, the "soliloquies" of Augustine as well, are fundamentally different from the "consciousness" that as self-consciousness, i.e., as self-certainty, constitutes the essence of the modern concept of truth, and that means of objectness and actuality. Hegel says in his lecture on the history of modern philosophy, after discussing Francis Bacon and Jakob Böhme: "Only now do we in fact arrive at the philosophy of the modern world, and we begin it with Descartes. With him we properly enter into an autonomous philosophy that knows that it is the autonomous product of reason and that *self-consciousness* is an essential moment of truth. Here, we can say, we are at home; and like the mariner after a long voyage on the stormy sea, we can cry 'Land, ho!' Descartes is one of

---

16. Hermann Diehls, *Die Fragmente der Vorsokratiker*, Greek and German, fifth edition by Walther Kranz (Berlin, 1934). Volume I, 173. [English: Heraclitus, *Fragments*, trans. T. M. Robinson (Toronto: University of Toronto Press, 1987), 61. "I investigated myself (or: I made enquiry of myself)."]

those people who started everything over again; and with him the formation, the thinking of the modern age begins."[17] "In this new period, the principle is *thinking*, the thinking that proceeds from itself."[18]

In our language we can also say: being an object of consciousness is now the essence of the being of all beings. All being is objectness of "consciousness." Modern metaphysics is what it is in the element of consciousness. If for a brief moment Hegel titled this work in which modern metaphysics consummates itself *Science of the Experience of Consciousness,* then we must not let the brightness of this moment pass by but must attempt to use this brightness to illuminate the work. We must especially not evade this necessity, because even though the title disappears again, there is talk of "experience" everywhere in the course of the work in its decisive passages. So we ask: What does "experience" mean in the domain of absolute metaphysics and its unconditional speculation? What does "experience of consciousness" mean?

On the present occasion, the elucidation of the title *Science of the Experience of Consciousness* on the basis of the introduction cannot be carried out by means of a formal, continuous interpretation of the text of the introduction as it should really be done. An overview, and that means an insight into the structure of the "Introduction," must provisionally suffice. The "Introduction" consists of sixteen paragraphs (1–16) which we will organize into five parts (I–V). At this time we will elucidate only the first four parts (1–15).

---

17. G. W. F. Hegel, *Vorlesungen über die Geschichte der Philosophie.* WW XV, ed. Karl Ludwig Michelet (Berlin, 1836), 328. [English: *Lectures on the History of Philosophy,* trans. Elizabeth S. Haldane and Frances H. Simpson (London: Kegan Paul, 1892–1896), 3:217.]

18. Ibid. [*Lectures on the History of Philosophy,* 3:217.]

I. THE GROUNDING OF THE ENACTMENT OF THE PRESENTATION OF APPEARING KNOWLEDGE (PARAGRAPHS 1–4 OF THE "INTRODUCTION")

Philosophy, i.e., metaphysics, deals with the cognition of what truly is, or with what beings truly are. For the metaphysics of German idealism, what truly is a being [*wahrhaft Seiende*] is the absolute. If in this metaphysics the absolute is to be cognized, this undertaking stands in the shadow of the philosophy of Kant, whose *Critique of Pure Reason* has the intention of creating clarity about the essence of the speculative cognition of the absolute by means of a well-grounded drawing of boundaries. The self-assurance of the procedure and of every attitude is a basic trait of modern philosophy in general. The act of carrying out an examining consideration about cognition itself *prior to* the cognition of the absolute is consistent with a "natural assumption" of this age.

Since Hegel wants to "introduce," he has to draw on a "natural assumption." Such instances where Hegel "draws on" a natural assumption can therefore be found throughout the entire "Introduction" to such an extent that Hegel begins every new step of the "Introduction" by "drawing on" a natural assumption. He does this in order to show to what extent the established views *appear* to be right but in fact are not. To speak more plainly and to use Hegel's language: What the established views mean by a prior examination of cognition before cognition means in fact something else.

Thus, Hegel by no means denies that the consummate cognition of the absolute has to be preceded by an "examination" of cognition. However, the type of this examination and the essence of the cognition of the absolute that is subjected to this examination can be determined only, if it can be determined at all, from the absolute itself.

If we begin the examination of cognition and of its faculty in the usual manner, we thereby already possess a concept of cognition. The latter serves as a "tool" with which we tackle the object that is to be cognized. But in order to be able to decide on the suitability or unsuitability of this tool we must already have cognized the object that is to be cognized. The cognizing relationship to the absolute is already presupposed. The same holds true if cognition is taken not as a "tool" but as a "medium" through which the light of truth reaches us. "Tool" and "medium" both have the character of a means. If, however, we take the cognition of the absolute as a means, then we *mis*recognize the essence and the sense of absolute cognition and of the absolute. For it is the essence of the absolute to include in itself everything that is relative and every relation to what is relative and thus also every relation of the relative to the absolute; because otherwise it would not be the absolute. The absolute can, therefore, never be something that we could first bring closer to ourselves through any kind of "tool," as if the absolute could at first *not* be with us. The absolute as absolute *is* "both in and for itself already with us," yes indeed, "it wants to be with us" (WW II, 60 [§73]).[1, [10]] By the same token, cognition is not a medium between us and the absolute, namely in such a way that cognition would amount to the refraction of the ray of cognition by the medium. Cognition is rather "the ray itself through which the truth touches us" (ibid. [§73]).

Almost in passing and hidden away in subordinate clauses, Hegel introduces in the first paragraph of the "Introduction" the idea that supports his metaphysics: The absolute is already with us and wants to be with us. Cognition is the ray of the absolute that touches us, not an undertaking that we carry out "afterward" in the direction of the absolute. We should know from the genuine recollection in the history of metaphysics that the latter, since the time of Plato and Aristotle, thinks beings only as beings by thinking at the same time the highest being (τιμιώτατον ὄν = τὸ θεῖον), and this as the ground and the originary cause [*Ur-sache*] (ἀρχή—αἴτιον) of all beings and thus of being. By thinking beings as beings (ὄν ᾗ ὄν), metaphysics is ontological. By thinking beings as beings from the highest being, metaphysics is theological. Metaphysics is in its essence ontotheological. This holds true not only for Plato's metaphysics and the metaphysics of Aristotle, let alone only for Christian metaphysics. Modern metaphysics is from Descartes to Nietzsche also ontotheology. The grounding and the evidence of the principle of self-certainty of the *ego cogito* has its foundation in the *idea innata substantiae infinitae*, i.e., *Dei*. Each monad

---

1. Note from the German editor: The quotations from the Phenomenology of Spirit are from hereafter cited according to the complete edition of Hegel's works (cf. above p.51, footnote 1 and 2) in abbreviated form after the quoted passage from the text.

sees the universe from a particular perspective and thus the divine central monad. According to Kant, all human reason, as the basic relation of man's essence to beings, is determined by the postulates of practical reason in which the existence of the highest good is posited as the unconditioned. And even being as the "will to power" is, according to Nietzsche, possible only on the basis of *the* unconditioned, which he can express only as "the eternal recurrence of the same."

Insofar as Hegel says: The absolute is already with us, and: cognition is the ray of the absolute that touches us, he says the same thing. At the same time, however, he says the same thing differently— namely, from a final unconditionedness that he posits as the first principle. We must finally comprehend this explicit and first cognizant positing of the first presupposition of all ontotheologically determined metaphysics for what it is. It is the highest resoluteness of the critical (transcendental) mindfulness concerning oneself that started with Descartes and that Kant first brought into the domain of metaphysics. It is the opposite of boundless speculation that leaves behind the boundary-posts of the critique. The knowledge of the essence of absolute knowledge knows itself already as absolute knowledge. It is knowledge in its essentiality, "the" science pure and simple, which alone can and must know its own essence. It is "the doctrine of science." This is according to Fichte the German and modern name for absolute metaphysics. This metaphysics is not a decline from the "critique," but it comprehends "critique" itself in its unconditionedness. It bears in mind that the highest thoughtfulness with respect to the cognition of the absolute consists in taking seriously in advance *that* which is cognized here. If, however, "the science" expresses itself thoughtlessly about the absolute and the cognition of the absolute, it simply comes on the scene in the midst of everyday opinion and among the appearing facts as one among others. But the mere coming on the scene and the pushing itself to the front is not a demonstration. Accordingly, Hegel says near the end of the first part of the "Introduction" (paragraph 4): "But science, just because it comes on the scene, is itself an appearance: in coming on the scene it is not yet science in its developed and unfolded truth" (WW II, 62 [§76]).

A mere coming on the scene would be contrary to the essence of absolute knowledge. If it appears at all, this appearance has to present itself in such a way that in this presentation the absolute brings its own appearing essence absolutely to appearance. But to appear absolutely means: to show the full essence completely in this appearance, namely in such a way that in this appearance above all the space and the ether, i.e., the "element" of appearance, also and simultaneously comes to appearance. However, the element in which absolute spirit shows itself as absolute knowledge is "consciousness." It is appearing knowledge in its appearance.

The presentation of appearing knowledge is necessary in order to carry the coming on the scene of "the science," i.e., of the systematic cognition of the absolute, beyond the mere coming on the scene in an undetermined element, and thus to allow the appearance of the absolute to be according to its essence, i.e., to be absolute.

The cognition of the absolute is now neither a tool nor a medium that lies outside of the absolute and that is separated from it; as consciousness, the cognition of the absolute is the element of its appearance that is grounded in the absolute itself and that is unfolded by the absolute, and it *is* this appearance in its various shapes. The cognition of the absolute is not a "means" but the course[11] of the appearing absolute itself through its different stages of appearance to itself. This amounts neither to a critique of the faculty of cognition nor to a contingent description of modes of cognition, but it is the self-presentation of the absolute itself in the element of its appearance that thereby opens up for the first time.

The absolute never is and never appears by merely coming on the scene among other things and somewhere, and that means relative to something that it is not itself. The absolute appears essentially only absolutely, i.e., in absolving[12] the totality of its stages of appearance; through this absolving it accomplishes the absolution, the release [*Lossprechung*] from the mere semblance of merely coming on the scene. This liberating accomplishment ("absolving") of its appearance may be called the absolvence of the absolute. The absolute "is" only in the mode of absolvence. The cognition of the absolute is never a means that tackles the absolute, i.e., it is never something relative, but it is—when it is—rather itself absolute, i.e., absolvent, i.e., it is a course and a path of the absolute to itself.

Therefore, in the following parts we will repeatedly speak of a "path" and we will characterize the self-presentation of the appearing spirit as a *course*.

II. THE SELF-PRESENTATION OF APPEARING KNOWLEDGE AS THE COURSE INTO THE TRUTH OF ITS OWN ESSENCE (PARAGRAPHS 5–8 OF THE "INTRODUCTION")

If we understand cognition in the manner of everyday representation as a course, and if we hear about the course of consciousness to its essential truth, i.e., to spirit, then we can indeed conceive all this "from the standpoint" of natural consciousness as a "path of the soul" to absolute spirit. The course is, then, an *Itinerarium mentis in Deum* (Bonaventura). Indeed, all attempts that have been undertaken so far to interpret Hegel's *Phenomenology of Spirit* have conceived of it in the sense of such a course that "natural consciousness" passes through. However, Hegel explicitly says (paragraph 5 [§77]) that one "can" conceive of the *Phenomenology of Spirit* from the standpoint of natural, i.e., non-philosophical consciousness in this manner. This means, however, precisely that this conception is philosophically untrue. For we are not dealing with a path that lies before natural consciousness and that it wanders on as wayfarer in the direction of the absolute. The course that Hegel has in mind is rather *the* course that the absolute itself goes, namely in such a way that in this course the absolute wends its way to its goal: the truth of its complete appearance. In this process, natural consciousness shows itself as a knowledge that has not yet actualized in itself the truth of knowing and therefore has to give up its obstinacy. But here everyday opinion again pushes itself to the front and grasps this path of consciousness to its truth and certainty in the manner of Descartes as a path of doubt. At most, however, the path of doubt, once it has passed through that which can be doubted, aims at obtaining and securing the matter again in the same way that it was before the occurrence of the doubt. The path of doubt becomes simply set on *the* certainty that the doubt, as the belief in itself and in its right, already presupposes. But the course of appearing knowledge to its essential truth is a course on which the first step already thinks toward the *essence* of consciousness, yet in doing this it must recognize that the essence that it grasps first, taken by itself, offers no hope of bringing the absolute in its truth, i.e., as absolvent and absolved, to appearance. The first step on the course of the absolute, which brings itself to appearance, demands another, to which, in turn, the same applies; and this continues as long as the totality of the essential shapes of consciousness has not yet been absolved; it is in this absolving alone that it is absolute. The course of appearing knowledge is thus from one step to the next rather a "path of despair" (paragraph 6, WW II, 63 [§78]). Even though the previous stages have to be given up, they must at the same time be preserved if the absolving is to be not a loss but the unique form of the attainment of the absolute. "The path of despair," however, would only be a path into what is without prospect on which nothing ever appears again. By constantly absolving and giving up these previous stages we thus necessarily go into these stages so that the current essential shape of consciousness can be taken up; for these shapes can be preserved in this progression only to the extent that they have been taken up. The course of appearing knowledge is a sublation of its essential shapes that come to appearance. This "sublation" is threefold: The shapes of consciousness that have been traversed not only are each taken up in the sense of a *tollere* (to pick up from the ground), they are at the same time preserved [*aufgehoben*] in the sense of *conservare* (to preserve). This preservation is a transmission in which consciousness gives itself over to those of its shapes that it has traversed, namely by picking them up and by preserving them in the essential succession of their appearance, whereby it "sublates" them in a double sense. Consciousness, presenting itself, thus realizes its appearance in a history, a history that serves the formation of its essence, namely in such a manner that in this formation consciousness knows itself in the completeness of its appearance. "The series of shapes that consciousness traverses on this path is rather the detailed history of the *formation* of consciousness to the standpoint of science" (paragraph 6, WW II, 64 middle [§78]).

Everyday opinion now again pushes itself to the front with a question. If the self-presentation of appearing knowledge is a course in the sense of the history of formation of the shapes of consciousness that we have characterized, from where does this course take the principle of the completeness of the shapes and from where does it take its goal at all and thus the rule of the succession of steps of the progression? Hegel responds to these questions in paragraphs 7 and 8. However, the answer to these questions that non-philosophical opinion poses can consist only in that the questions themselves are to be "posed correctly," as it is the case everywhere in this "Introduction." This happens in the form of the suggestion that these questions of ordinary opinion do not ask with a view to *that* which alone is in question: the absolute and the cognition of the absolute.

The course is the course of appearing knowledge to its essence that is with it itself. The goal of this course lies neither outside the course nor at its end. The goal is the beginning from which the course begins and takes each of its steps. The shapes of consciousness do not follow each other in such a way that the final shape appears last, but the first shape as such is rather already a shape of the absolute; it is in advance raised up [*hinaufgehoben*] (*elevare*) into the absoluteness of the absolute. Put differently: The absolute determines what appears as the first stage of the appearance of the essence of the absolute. If the *Phenomenology of Spirit* "begins" with *sense certainty* and "ends" with *absolute spirit*, as is outwardly indicated by the table of contents of the work, then this beginning in sense certainty is not posited out of consideration for the human being who at first lingers in this mode of knowing. The *Phenomenology of Spirit* rather begins with the appearance of the *essence* of sense certainty because this shape of knowledge is the outermost externalization into which the absolute is able to release itself. If, however, it releases itself into this shape, then as far as the shapes of its essence are concerned it is with the emptiest and poorest shape, and is thus the farthest away from its own completeness. This essential distancing from itself is the basic condition for the absolute to give itself the possibility—out of itself and for itself—of traversing a course that is the return to itself. If the course of absolute knowledge to itself, as the passage through the essential shapes of its appearance, has the basic trait of sublation, then this sublation is according to its proper and underlying essence before all an elevation—a being-raised up into the absolute. Let us not forget what seem to be only passing remarks in the first paragraph: The absolute is already with us, i.e., it is already in the most primitive shape of consciousness, and our cognition is the ray that touches us as the absolute truth.

In paragraph 8, which characterizes the goal of the course of consciousness, Hegel says: "Consciousness, however, is for itself its own *concept*" (WW II, 66 [§80]). Consciousness is according to its essence self-consciousness. However, self-consciousness is its essence, i.e., it is *for* itself what it is, only to the extent that it knows itself as self-consciousness in the completeness of its essence. According to Hegel, this self-knowing knowledge of itself is "the concept."

Since consciousness only is by being its concept, it is—insofar as it is this constant bringing-itself-before-itself—in its essential shapes a constant being-wrested beyond itself by itself to itself. "Thus consciousness suffers this violence of spoiling its own limited satisfaction {i.e., having to transcend each of its stages in despair} at its own hands" (ibid. [§80]).

As this being-wrested into the domain of truth of its own essence, consciousness itself comes "out" as that which it is in its appearance. It presents itself. It is presentation and "is" as such. The course of the self-presentation of consciousness into the interrelated stages of its shapes has the basic trait of *sublation* in the threefold sense of taking up (*tollere*), preserving (*conservare*), and raising up (*elevare*) that we have characterized. The third of these modes of sublation, the raising up into the consummate essence of consciousness (i.e., into its truth and "actuality") is the first and underlying one in the whole of the sublation according to the matter [*Sache*] and to the "essence." Consciousness essentially occurs as self-consciousness in advance in the elevation to the absolute. And it takes up its object-of-consciousness always only out of the elevation, so that within this elevation it can preserve the consciousness of what it is conscious of as a shape.

From another point of view one characterizes the mere taking up and ascertaining of the object-of-consciousness as thesis; the taking back of that which is thus posited for consciousness as an object-of-consciousness into self-consciousness as antithesis; and the taking together of the two into the higher unity as synthesis. If one thinks in the order of succession of everyday opinion, the course of consciousness comes from the thesis, goes over to the antithesis, and goes up to the synthesis. Given this progression, one now asks Hegel how a guiding thread for the progression from the thesis to the antithesis and from both of these to the synthesis can be discerned at all. In the everyday representation of this course one does indeed not find a guiding thread for this progression—and rightfully so. One thus develops some misgivings and reaches the objection and reproach against Hegel that he stages, indeed that he even has to stage the progression as a triad out of pure arbitrariness. For if at first only the thesis is posited, any indication of the direction and the domain from which the antithesis is to be taken is still missing. And when the latter is posited, it still remains questionable in what respect the contraposition is to be comprehended as a composition and a unity.

Yet this critique of Hegel's thinking, which is often enough brought up also from the "philosophical" camp, does not think philosophically at all. It completely overlooks the fact that the synthesis is what supports and guides, and that the domain of that which deserves the *conservare* and that therefore demands a *tollere* is already circumscribed by the violence of the elevation that prevails before everything else. In order to be able to bring the course of consciousness in its appearance to presentation, the thinking that presents it must before all think the synthesis, and only from out of the synthesis it must think the thesis and the antithesis. Yet insofar as this synthesis is absolute, it is not "made" by us; we only carry it out. The synthesis and the absolute elevation is already as that which Hegel mentions in the first paragraph of the "Introduction" when he says these two things: The absolute is already with us; cognition is the ray by which the truth (the absolute) itself touches us. If one disregards this by misrecognizing "the (absolute) violence" (WW II, 60 [§73][13]) that already prevails in the essence of consciousness, then every attempt to follow the course of consciousness in thought and to know the inner law of the progression of the course is futile.

Conversely, the following holds true as well: If we think in advance from the primordial elevation and synthesis of consciousness, then the ground for determining the type of progression and thus the totality of the shapes that are to be traversed is already given. Until consciousness knows itself unconditionally and in its truth, and thus is its own self in and for itself, the violence of its absolute essence coerces consciousness to progress. Every shape of the progression and the transition from one to the next is now determined by the goal of the course: They are the shapes and stages of self-consciousness that determine themselves with regard to absolute self-consciousness. The negation of the previous shape that is carried out in the progression is not an empty negating. Viewed from the sublated stage, the latter is not just put aside and given up; nor does the negation, when viewed from the perspective of the progression, go into an empty indeterminacy. The negation that takes place in the progression, and thus its essence, is "determinate negation." Hegel discusses this in paragraph 7 of the "Introduction."

Since the course is supported and guided by the elevation, the progression is a gradual ascent to ever higher stages. And since this ascending progression is in itself a differentiating transition from one stage to another, it becomes manifest that the course of the self-presentation of appearing knowledge that separates and differentiates the lower from the higher has the character of an *examination*.

Examination—in the age of Kant this sounds like an *"epistemological"* consideration of cognition, which for this purpose is isolated for itself like a "means." More importantly, common thought at once asks the question as to where the criterion [*Maßstab*] of this "examination" is taken from. By engaging, again, with what ordinary opinion thinks about measure-taking [*Maß-nehmen*] and about examinations, in the next part of the "Introduction" Hegel explains essential moments of the course of the self-presentation of appearing knowledge.

III. THE CRITERION OF THE EXAMINATION AND
THE ESSENCE OF THE EXAMINATION
IN THE COURSE OF APPEARING KNOWLEDGE
(PARAGRAPHS 9–13 OF THE "INTRODUCTION")

1. The criterion-forming consciousness and the
dialectical movement of the examination

We will let the questions about the criterion and the type of the examination of consciousness be answered by means of two sentences
by Hegel that we pick out from the third part of the "Introduction":
These two sentences about consciousness have *an inner connection* to
the sentence from paragraph 8 mentioned above (cf. above p.68) that
says that consciousness is the concept of itself. One of the sentences
can be found at the beginning of paragraph 12: "Consciousness furnishes its own criterion in it itself . . ." (WW II, 68 [§84]).

To what extent is consciousness as consciousness, and thus in itself,
criterion-like, namely in such a way that it furnishes the criterion that
accords to its essence already by being consciousness, i.e., that it "furnishes its own criterion in it itself"? Hegel deliberately says "in it itself"
[*an ihm selbst*], not: in itself [*an sich selbst*], in order to express the point
that consciousness does not need to develop after the fact and out of
itself. Hegel not only thinks consciousness in general in the sense of
Descartes as self-consciousness, so that all objects-of-consciousness
are what they *are* for an I, i.e., something that stands over and against
representation (object). At the same time, Hegel thinks consciousness
in advance "transcendentally" in the Kantian sense, i.e., with a view
to the objectness of the object of consciousness. But the objective of
the object is grounded in and determined by the originarily unifying (synthetic) functions of self-consciousness. They constitute the objectness of the object so that every object as such, i.e., with respect
to its objectness, has to measure itself against self-consciousness, i.e.,

against the essence of consciousness. This is the only sense of the idea that Kant expresses in the preface to the second edition of his *Critique of Pure Reason* (B XVI [110])—an idea that is often quoted and that is equally often misinterpreted and equally often quoted only partially—in which he compares his transcendental inquiry with the inquiry of Copernicus. The sentences read: "Thus far it has been assumed that all our cognition must conform to objects; but all attempts to find out something about them *a priori* through concepts, whereby our cognition would be expanded, have, on this presupposition, come to nothing. Hence let us try to see whether we do not make better progress with the tasks of metaphysics if we assume that objects must conform to our cognition, which would agree better with the demanded possibility of an *a priori* cognition of them that is to ascertain something about objects before they are given to us. This would be just like the first thought of *Copernicus,* who, having difficulties in making progress in the explanation of the celestial motions when he assumed that the entire host of stars revolves around the observer, tried to see if he might not have greater success if he had the observer revolve and the stars remain at rest."[14]

This comparison does not at all sound like a "subjectivism" as it is conceived by common thought. The spectator ought to revolve around the stars, not the stars around the spectator. Kant mentions this in order to elucidate his own inquiry by means of a comparison with the Copernican turn. But does Kant not say that the object ought to conform to our cognition, and thus the stars to the spectator? No—let us read closely. Kant says: The objects ought to conform *"to our cognition,"* i.e., to the *essence* of consciousness. That is to say: Kant leaves beings in themselves alone and yet determines them in such manner that he lets appearance, and thus the spectator who represents that which appears, revolve around the thing itself. Kant does *not* want to say: That tree over there, as a tree, must conform to what I, here, think of it; but that the tree as an object has the essence of its objectness in that which belongs in advance to the essence of objectness. *This* objectness is the criterion of the object, which means that the originary unity of self-consciousness and its unifying representation is *the* criterion of the object-of-consciousness as such; this criterion is given in the essence of self-consciousness. Hegel says: Consciousness furnishes its own criterion in it itself because it always already expresses itself about the objectness of its object, and that means it expresses itself about itself. Unlike Kant, Hegel does not stop at human self-consciousness but explicitly makes even self-consciousness itself its own object, thus letting the more originary criteria unfold in it. Insofar as Kant makes assertions about the essence of self-consciousness that are measured against the essence of reason in general, he effectively already proceeds like Hegel. However, Hegel's proposition: "Consciousness furnishes its own criterion in it itself," does not only say that the criterion is given immediately with the essence of consciousness and that it lies *in* this essence; by saying "furnishes," he says at the same time that on its course to *its essence* consciousness each time lets its own criterion appear, and thus it is in itself *criterion-forming*. This criterion changes at every stage insofar as the originary elevation into the absolute and thus the absolute itself appears step by step as the completeness of the essence of consciousness. Consciousness comports itself as such to what it is conscious of (the "object"), and in referring the object to *itself* as *its own self* it also already comports *itself to itself*.[15] The object is thus what it is *for* self-consciousness. But the latter as well is what it is by appearing to itself: namely as that which constitutes the objectness of the object. Self-consciousness *is* in itself the criterion of its object. By comporting itself *to* the object, as that which is to be measured, at the same time, however, to itself, as that which does the measuring, in this twofold comportment self-consciousness carries out within itself the comparison of what is to be measured and its criterion. *For it,* as one and the same, are at the same time what is to be measured and what does the measuring. Consciousness *is* in itself essentially *this comparison*. And insofar as it *is* in itself this comparison, *it is essentially examination*. Consciousness carries out the *examination* of its essence not occasionally in critical situations but all the time insofar as it thinks as self-consciousness in the direction of its essence, and that means in the direction of the objectness of the object. Hegel thus says: Consciousness examines itself (compare paragraph 13, WW II, 69 [§85]). Just as the criterion of the examination does not need to be supplied to consciousness from somewhere or other, neither is the examination carried out on it only by us and from time to time. The course of consciousness into its own appearing essence is in itself at the same time criterion-forming and criterion-examining. Therefore, consciousness is *in itself a confrontation with itself*.

However, the course of consciousness has the basic trait of *sublation* in which consciousness itself exposes itself into the truth of its essence and brings its essential shapes to appearance in the unity of an essential history. Consciousness is confrontation [*Auseinandersetzung*] in a double sense: On the one hand, it is a disputing, examining laying-itself-asunder [*Sichauseinanderlegen*], a disputation with itself. As this laying-asunder, it is and it lays itself out and interprets itself, and it is this self-exposition in the unity of that which is gathered in itself.[16] In Greek, the essence of the exposing, revealing gathering is the λέγειν. The essence of λόγος is δηλοῦν, ἀποφαίνεσθαι, ἑρμηνεύειν. Aristotle's treatise on λόγος therefore bears the title Περὶ ἑρμηνείας (that means: On the letting-appear that lays asunder). {The inner relation to ἰδέα and ἰδεῖν and to εἰδέναι is obvious.} The exposition that lays asunder in the unity of the conversation that confronts is the διάλογος—the διαλέγεσθαι. The medial term captures the double meaning of διά as "through" and "between" and denotes the dialogue of a self-expression that runs through a subject matter and *thus* brings this subject matter to appearance. The self-expression about the being of beings is already for Plato a dialogue of the soul with itself. The dialogical-agonic essence of διαλέγεσθαι returns in a modified, modern, and unconditioned form in Hegel's determination of the essence of consciousness. As the threefold sublating, thetic-antithetic-synthetic, and criterion-forming examination, the course of consciousness is "dialectical" in the originary sense. The course of consciousness that it works out on it itself [*an ihm selbst*] is a "dialectical movement." In the first thirteen paragraphs the essence of the course of the consciousness that presents itself has been clarified so far and in such a unified manner that in paragraph 14, which makes up the fourth part, Hegel can move on to the decisive proposition of the "Introduction."

2. Review of the previous discussion (I–III)

Since Hegel expresses the basic trait of the essence of the *Phenomenology of Spirit* in the three subsequent and final paragraphs of the "Introduction," it is advisable to review our elucidation of the "Introduction" up to this point in summary form. At the beginning of the elucidation of Hegel's *Phenomenology of Spirit* we pointed out the varied role and position of the *Phenomenology* in Hegel's metaphysics. In the first system, which calls itself *System of Science,* the *Phenomenology of Spirit* constitutes the first part of the system under the title *Science of the Phenomenology of Spirit.* "Science," without any qualification, means here: "philosophy." The title *System of Science* means "philosophy" in the shape of the developed "system," which is its only suitable shape. Philosophy, as the unconditioned, all-conditioning knowledge, is in itself "systematic"; it is only what it is as a "system." (This name names the essential structure *of* science itself, not the conventional form of a subsequent ordering of philosophical knowledge.) Due to the all-determining role that the *Phenomenology* plays in the first two-part system it may be called the "Phenomenology-system." The second, three-part system, which must have gained primacy soon after the appearance of the *Phenomenology of Spirit,* knows the *Phenomenology of Spirit* only as a subordinate part of the third main part. What the disappearance of the *Phenomenology of Spirit* from the role of the first part of the system signifies for the system itself, and thus for the metaphysics of German Idealism, can only be gauged, in fact it can only clearly be asked, when the essence of the *Phenomenology of Spirit* has been sufficiently clarified. We are here attempting to take a few steps in the direction of this clarification, and we will do so on a simple path.

What is the *Phenomenology of Spirit*? We take the answer to this question from the "Introduction" that Hegel places between the actual work and the more extensive "Preface." What does the "Introduction" introduce and how does it do so? It is the preparation of the approach to the leap into the thinking that thinks in this work. The preparation of the leap is carried out by way of the elucidation of the title *Science of the Experience of Consciousness*. This title, however, is missing in the work published in 1807 and likewise in the publication of 1832. The proper purpose of the "Introduction" is therefore not plain to see. After Fichte's *Doctrine of Science,* it is understandable that Hegel names an essential part of the *System of Science* "science." It is also not surprising that the system of modern metaphysics, which has found its ground and foundation in "consciousness," thematizes "consciousness." The characterization of metaphysics as "science of consciousness" also makes sense. In contrast, what is surprising is that the word "experience" appears in the title of a work of absolute speculative metaphysics; because the "empirical" is precisely that which in all metaphysics, not only in modern metaphysics, remains inessential and remains precisely in need of the essentiality of the essence.

The clarification of the concept of "experience" in the title *Science of the Experience of Consciousness* has to hit the center of the elucidation and thus has to hit the core of the explanation of the essence of the *Phenomenology of Spirit*. That which is unique about this work arises from the basic position that Western metaphysics had reached in the meantime. Metaphysics is the cognition of the totality of beings as such from their ground. It cognizes that which truly is a being in its truth. According to the onto-theological essence of metaphysics, that which truly is a being is the being that is most in being (*ens entium*), that which alone is from and through itself: the absolute. The "final end" (Kant) of metaphysical cognition is the cognition of the absolute. Only the metaphysics of German Idealism has recognized clearly and decisively that the cognition "of" the absolute can be so only if it cognizes at the same time in an absolute *manner*. Metaphysics' claim of absolute knowledge must now be comprehended in its essential necessity. This claim must justly demonstrate its rightfulness because it essentially reaches beyond the boundaries of the everyday cognition of finite things. It must be examined if and how cognition *can* be such

an *absolute* cognition. In accordance with modern thought's own epis-
temic stance, this examination is completely inevitable; because for
modern thought "truth" means self-demonstrating certainty without
doubt. *Absolute* metaphysics can therefore the least elude the demand
for an "examination" and a demonstration. But the decisive question
is what sort of examination the examination of absolute cognition
alone can be and how it must be carried out. For if cognition is being
examined, then there already exists a prior opinion about the essence
of the cognition that is to be examined, prior to the enactment of this
examination. And the common view of cognition holds that cognition
is either a "tool" or a "medium" and thus in any case a "means" that
lies between the cognizer and the cognized, and that is neither one
nor the other. If, however, the cognition of absolute cognition were a
mere "means," then it would remain "outside" the absolute and thus
would not be absolute. But as "something relative," cognition always
stands in relation to . . . , it is related to the absolute. It is therefore in
any case necessary to focus immediately and in advance on *this relation* to the absolute and to lay it down as the essence of cognition. Provided that we think the absolute as the absolute, cognition's relation
to the absolute can *only* be the relation *of* the absolute *to us,* the cog-
nizers. It belongs to the thoughtful art of Hegel's thoughtful power of
presentation that he mentions this essence of absolute cognition in
the "Introduction" almost only in passing in subordinate clauses toward the end of the first paragraph. Formulated in the form of guiding propositions, Hegel says the following about the absolute and the
cognition of the absolute:

1. The absolute is in and for itself already with us and wants to be
with us (cf. WW II, 60 [§73]).

2. Cognition is "the ray itself through which the truth touches us"
(ibid. [§73]).

With respect to the necessity of the examination we must now ask:
What is absolute cognition if it cannot be a "means"? And: Of what
sort is the examination if it does not need to examine a "means" with
respect to its suitability?

If cognition, our cognition, is essentially the ray by which the absolute touches us, then cognition, viewed from our standpoint, proves
to be a radiating that we who have been touched by the ray radiate
back, so that in this reverse ray we can follow the ray that touches us
in its opposite direction. Cognition is thus no longer a "means" but
a "path." *This* basic trait of cognition, which announces itself as ὁδός
(μέθοδος) since the beginning of Western metaphysics, is repeatedly
mentioned in the "Introduction" to the *Phenomenology of Spirit.* Hegel
thus determines in what sense the cognition of the absolute has the

basic trait of a "path." This is done in the service of the task of the "Introduction" that consists in constantly starting from common views while, at the same time, making visible their *un*suitability. At first one could indeed still say: The characterization of cognition as path likewise considers cognition as means. After all, we speak of "the means" and "paths" in the same phrase.

But if cognition is the ray, then the path cannot be a "stretch" that exists for itself between the absolute and us and thus is distinguished from both. There is nothing between us and the absolute except the absolute itself, which comes toward us *as a ray*. We can grasp this coming [of the absolute] only by traveling it ourselves as a course; that is, by coming toward it. But this course never begins by taking place away from, i.e., outside, the absolute, so that it will eventually reach the latter; instead, the course is in advance already with the absolute in the sense of the originary synthesis of the elevation where it is radiated upon by the ray. The synthesis alone determines the stages of the course, and thus the progression and the totality of its states are determined. Insofar as the movement is the unfolding of the synthesis, it has the character of a thetic-antithetic succession of steps, i.e., the character of the "dialectical" path.

Absolute cognition must be examined. In the examination cognition must prove that it is what it claims to be. If, however, the cognition of the absolute is the ray by which the absolute touches us, then the absolute—if this manner of speaking is at all still permitted—can prove that it is the absolute *only by* appearing out of itself, and by thereby manifesting this appearance as its essence. The absolute is spirit, or put in modern terms: it is unconditioned self-consciousness. Consciousness is unconditioned self-comprehension. The first proposition "of" consciousness reads: "Consciousness . . . is for itself its own *concept*" (paragraph 8, WW II, 66 [§80]). In self-comprehension, absolute knowledge brings itself to appearance in accordance with its essence. The absolute *is* as consciousness essentially *the* appearing knowledge. Our examination of absolute cognition can thus no longer be an accomplishment that tackles cognition as if the latter were a means that was somewhere present-at-hand. Since cognition itself is the irradiated course to that which radiates, the essence of the examination, which becomes possible only here, fulfils itself in that it is this course *itself* in a determinate manner. This course must let the appearing knowledge show itself in its appearance, i.e., in its own truth. On this course the absolute comes to us as the appearing consciousness that unfolds itself in the truth of its essence. It proves that it is the absolute by exhibiting itself and thus shows that *in* this appearance it is commensurate with its essence that shows itself in this appearance. This implies: The examination does not need to supply the criterion that it requires.

The second proposition "of" consciousness says: "Consciousness furnishes its own criterion {i.e., the truth of its essence} in it itself" (paragraph 12, W W II, 68 [§80]). And so long as consciousness appears essentially and this appearance is an examination in the sense of such an "exhibiting," the third proposition "of" consciousness holds true: Consciousness examines itself (paragraph 13, W W II, 69 [§85]). What remains for us is only "the pure looking on" during the appearance of consciousness, which is a movement that consciousness exercises on it itself. It remains to be seen in what manner we, as the ones who examine, are ourselves the enactment of the performance of this movement. We must comprehend what Hegel understands by the "experience of consciousness."

3. The experience [Er-fahren] of consciousness[17]

Even though Kant designates as "experience" that which according to Aristotle is essentially distinct from ἐμπειρία, namely the acquaintance [Kenntnis] with the διότι (i.e., of causality for Kant), both *agree* that "experience" and ἐμπειρία refer to *beings* that are immediately accessible in their everydayness, and that both are thus modes of cognizance [Kenntnisnahme] and cognition.

What Hegel calls "experience" in the *Phenomenology of Spirit* refers neither to beings that are perceptible in their everydayness, nor to beings at all; nor is "experience," strictly speaking, a mode of cognition.

If, for Hegel, "the experience" is *not* any of this, then what is it? For Hegel experience is "the experience of consciousness." But what does that mean? We will now attempt to name the essential moments of experience (seemingly in the form of an external list) with constant reference to the elucidation of the "Introduction" that has been given so far.

Experience is "the dialectical movement." Experience is a journeying [Fahren] (*pervagari*) that traverses a "path." But the path does not in itself lie before the journeying. The path is a course in the double sense of the activity of going (going to the countryside) and of a passageway (subterranean passageway).[18] More precisely, the course as a passage is only experienced [er-fahren] in the course as a going, i.e., it is explored [er-gangen], and that is to say: it is opened up so that what is manifest can show itself. That which travels this going und the opening of this passageway is consciousness as re-presentation.

The placing-before-oneself goes ahead and opens up and presents, and only thereby it becomes the ether of the self-showing and appearance.

Experience, conceived as this course (*pervagari*), is at the same time experience in the originary sense of πεῖρα. This means the involvement with something out of the intention of seeing what comes out of it.[19] This involvement with what has not yet appeared as what is not yet decided has its essential location in the domain of competition where it means: the involvement with an opponent, the "taking on" of the same. Experience as *probare* is an examination that aims at that which it has to expect on its course as course.

Experience as this course of the examination examines consciousness with regard to that which it is itself, with regard to its essence against which it constantly measures itself as self-consciousness. This weighing experience is not directed toward beings but being, namely being-conscious.[20] Experience is not ontic but ontological, or to use Kant's language: it is transcendental experience.

However, as *probare* and *pervagari* this transcendental measuring and weighing (*librare*) is a course that examines and goes over the essential succession of the shapes of consciousness, and that means it goes through this essential succession. Experience is a "going through"; for one in the sense of *enduring and suffering*, namely of the violence of its own absolute essence that essentially occurs in consciousness. The *going through* is a being-wrested into the essential height of the concealed and unconditioned "elevation"; at the same time, however, this going through is a "passing" in the sense of absolving, of the passage through the totality of stages and shapes—predetermined from the elevation—of the being of consciousness.

As this ambiguous [*doppelsinnig*] going through, the experience of consciousness is the passage through the three senses of sublation. The negation of the thesis by the antithesis belongs to sublation in such a way that what is negated in this negation is preserved, and the negation of the antithesis is, in turn, negated by the synthesis. The going through has the basic trait of this originary double negation that demands a constant giving up of what has supposedly been achieved. The course of experience is a "path of despair," and therefore experience is essentially a "painful experience." Hegel always conceives of "pain" metaphysically, i.e., as a type of "consciousness," the consciousness of being-other, of the tearing, of negativity. The experience of consciousness is as a transcendental-dialectical experience always the "bad" experience in which the object of consciousness each time turns out to be different from what it appeared to be at first. The experience is the transcendental pain of consciousness. Insofar as the experience of consciousness is "pain" it is at the same time a going through in the sense of an elaboration [*Herausarbeiten*] of the essential shapes of appearing self-consciousness. To say that experience is the "labor of the concept" means that it is the self-elaboration of consciousness into the unconditioned totality of the truth of its self-comprehension. Experience is the transcendental labor that wears itself out [*abarbeiten*] in the service of the unconditioned violence of the absolute.[21] Experience is the transcendental labor of consciousness.

As a course, an examination, a going through (a carrying out and a consummation), pain, labor, the experience of consciousness is always also and everywhere a cognizance and a taking notice. But this taking notice is never a mere apprehension but the letting-appear that as course and journeying each time experiences [*er-fährt*], i.e., attains, an essential shape of consciousness.

Experience as attaining is, however, only the unfolding of consciousness into the truth of its being. The experience of consciousness is not only and not primarily a kind of cognition, but it is a being [*ein Sein*], namely the being of the appearing absolute whose own essence lies in unconditioned appearing to itself. For Hegel, the absolute is "the concept" in the sense of the unconditioned self-comprehension of reason. This unconditioned concept is the essence of spirit. Spirit is in itself and for itself "the absolute idea." "Idea" means: the showing of itself, but understood in modern terms: as representation of oneself to the one who represents—unconditioned representation [*Repräsentation*], manifestation of its own self in the unconditioned truth of its own essence, which in modern terms is certainty and knowledge. Spirit is absolute knowledge. The experience of consciousness is the self-presentation of knowledge in its appearance. "The experience of consciousness" is the essence of "phenomenology." Phenomenology, in turn, is "the phenomenology of spirit."

Only if we succeed at thinking the moments of the essence of experience mentioned here from the ground of their unity in a unified manner are we in the position to think the wording of the titles "the Experience *of* Consciousness" and "the Phenomenology of Spirit," truthfully, i.e., in a speculative and metaphysical way.

Linguistically both titles contain a genitive. We ask: Is the genitive a *genitivus objectivus* or a *genitivus subjectivus*? Does "the experience of consciousness" only mean that consciousness is the object [*Objekt*] of and what stands against [*Gegenstand*] experience? This is evidently not the case, because experience itself is in its essence as a course and a coming to itself the being of consciousness. "Experience" fully comprehended expresses for the first time what the word "being" in the word being-conscious [*Bewußt-sein*] means. Consciousness is the "subject" of experience; it is that which goes through the experience with itself. Therefore the genitive must be understood as a *genitivus subjectivus*. However, the essence of the subject as self-consciousness consists precisely in not only that consciousness is consciousness of something and has its object, but that it is itself object for itself. Therefore, the experience that consciousness goes through is at the same time the experience that it undergoes "with itself" as an object. The genitive is thus at the same time also a *genitivus objectivus*. And yet, the genitive is not simply both together, but it is a genitive that names the unity of the subject and the object and the ground of their unity, i.e., the elevation and synthesis in the metaphysical essence of consciousness. The genitive in the expressions "the experience of consciousness" and "the phenomenology of spirit" is the speculative-metaphysical genitive. All genitives of the language of the *Phenomenology of Spirit* belong to this type. In fact, not only the genitives but also the other cases and all inflections of the words have a speculative meaning. Only if we bear this in mind, and that means if we practice this, we can follow the web of this language, and that means we can understand the text.

It is even necessary to follow this instruction in order to think the complete title of the work correctly: *Science of the Experience of Consciousness, Science of the Phenomenology of Spirit*. The genitive "science of . . ." is speculative, i.e., the science not only deals *with* the experience of consciousness but consciousness is its subject, which supports and determines science. Science is cognition. But according to the proposition of the first paragraph of the introduction cognition is "the ray through which the truth touches us." Our cognition, i.e., the speculative thinking of the absolute, is only when and insofar as it is the ray, and that means insofar as it radiates itself while being radiated upon by the ray.

Across the essential transformations of modern metaphysics the same thing appears that Plato pronounces at the beginning of metaphysics: that the eye must be ἡλιοειδές. The sun is the image for the "idea of the good," i.e., for the unconditioned.

Since consciousness has the essence of its being in the "experience" that we have characterized, it examines itself and unfolds from itself the criteria of the examination. Therefore, what remains for us in the realization of this self-presentation of consciousness is a pure "*looking on*," and "a contribution by us is superfluous" (paragraph 13, WW II, 69 [§85]).

IV. THE ESSENCE OF THE EXPERIENCE OF CONSCIOUSNESS AND ITS PRESENTATION (PARAGRAPHS 14–15 OF THE "INTRODUCTION")

1. Hegel's "ontological" concept of experience

Paragraph 14 begins with the following words: "*Inasmuch as the new true object arises from it,* this *dialectical* movement that consciousness exercises on it itself, both on its knowing and its object, is what is genuinely called *experience*" (WW II, 70 [§86]). If the preceding deliberation has determined the essence of the dialectical course as the letting-appear of the essential shapes of consciousness, and if the absolute thus appears in the "dialectical movement," and *if* this essence of the "dialectical movement" truly constitutes the essence of "*experience,*" then Hegel's concept of "experience" *can*not be thrown together with the common concept of "empirical evidence" [*Empirie*]. ("Movement" as μεταβολὴ ἔκ τινος εἴς τι. Ἐνέργεια.[22] Cf. for "sense certainty" paragraph 8 [§80].) And yet it will become apparent that Hegel's concept of experience, and it alone and for the first time, thinks back into the concealed essential moments of experience that announce themselves at times also in the concept of experience of everyday "life," though they do so contingently and without unity. In order to bring out the peculiarities of Hegel's concept of experience with the necessary sharpness, we must keep in mind the traditional concept of "experience" in at least two of its main forms. Therefore we shall start by briefly recalling Aristotle's concept of ἐμπειρία and Kant's concept of "experience."

Aristotle determines what ἐμπειρία is in the first chapter of the first book of the *Metaphysics,* which begins with the sentence: Πάντες ἄνθρωποι τοῦ εἰδέναι ὀρέγονται φύσει.[23] All human beings have from the bottom of their essence a pre-dilection to bring to their sight (everything toward which they comport themselves), in order to have it present in its outward look (εἰδέναι—ἰδεῖν).[24] {What is not expressed or thought

through in this sentence, even though it is its foundation, is that the
human being essentially keeps beings present to himself as presence.}
The manners according to which the human being has what is present in sight are manifold. One of them is the ἐμπειρία. If, for example,
we are familiar[25] with the fact that every time someone falls ill with
such and such a disease a particular medicine helps, then the having-
before-oneself in advance of the matter, namely that "when this . . . ,
then that . . . ," is ἐμπειρία. Its essence consists in τὸ ἔχειν ὑπόληψιν—
having at one's disposal the fore-having of "if this . . . , then that. . . ."
It is characteristic of the ἐμπειρία that it remains merely the familiarity
with the existence of this "if this . . . , then in each case that. . . ." The
person who is familiar with such matters has in view *that* it is this way,
but he does not see into what makes for *why* it is the way it is. οἱ μὲν
γὰρ ἔμπειροι τὸ ὅτι μὲν ἴσασι, διότι δ'οὐκ ἴσασιν.[1] Those who are having
an experience have the that in sight, but they do not have (the) why
in sight (they lack insight). The having-in-sight of the why of a matter
is characteristic of the τέχνη; it is the essence of ἐπιστήμη—of science.

(The essential event, namely that at the beginning of Western metaphysics with Plato and Aristotle the essence of "science" (ἐπιστήμη)
develops out of the essence of τέχνη, corresponds in a concealed and
necessary way to another event, namely that at the end of Western
metaphysics (i.e., since the nineteenth century) the essence of modern
science comes to light and establishes itself as an essential form of
modern machine technology.)

That which for Aristotle is ἐμπειρία, the familiar fore-having of the
"If . . . , therefore . . . ," (If . . . , then . . .)-matter is for Kant *not* yet
an "experience" but a "perception." In the *Prolegomena* Kant mentions
the familiarity with the fact that every time the sun shines the stone
gets warm as an example of this kind of acquaintance with things.
We are dealing with an "experience" in the Kantian sense only when
this familiarity has essentially been transformed into a cognition: *Because* the sun shines, the stone gets warm. In addition to the perception, the proposition "The sun warms the stone" gives the new kind
of information of a sensibly perceptible and objective matter that is
valid for everyone, namely that of a cause-effect relationship. Kant
says: "Experience is an empirical cognition, i.e., a cognition that determines an object through perceptions. It is therefore a synthesis of
perceptions, which is not itself contained in perception but contains

---

1. *Aristotelis Metaphysica,* ed. Wilhelm von Christ (Leipzig: B. G. Teubner, 1886),
981a28ff. [English: *The Complete Works of Aristotle,* ed. Jonathan Barnes, vol. 2
(Princeton, N.J.: Princeton University Press, 1984). "For men of experience know
that the thing is so, but do not know why."]

the synthetic unity of the manifold of perception in one consciousness, whose {unity} constitutes what is essential in a cognition of *objects* of the senses, i.e., of experience (not merely of the intuition or sensation of the senses)" (*Critique of Pure Reason*, B218f. [295f.][26]). That which Kant conceives of as "experience" is actualized in the mathematical natural science in the Newtonian sense.

Hegel's concept of "experience" is essentially, and that means infinitely (and thus not simply in some respect), distinct from both Aristotle's ἐμπειρία and Kant's "experience." Although Kant, in contrast to Aristotle, conceives "experience" as that which according to Aristotle differs essentially from ἐμπειρία, namely the acquaintance [*Kenntnis*] with the διότι (in Kantian terms the representation of the cause-effect-synthesis), Aristotle *and* Kant *agree* that "experience" and ἐμπειρία refer to beings that are immediately accessible in their everydayness. In contrast, what Hegel calls "experience" refers neither to beings that are perceptible in their everydayness nor to beings at all, nor is "experience" strictly speaking a "cognition" [*Erkenntnis*] in the sense of a merely representing human comportment. What then is "experience" for Hegel? If experience is directed toward "anything" at all, what is its "object"?

According to the first sentence of paragraph 14 and especially according to the words that are letter-spaced,[27] "experience" is the letting-arise of the *"new* true object." This letting-arise is carried out by consciousness. The letting-arise thus proves to be a movement that consciousness exercises on itself. In this movement the object that arises therein is explicitly given back to consciousness, to whom it has belonged in a concealed manner all along, as its essential property. The final sentence of the paragraph even says: "This new object contains the nullity of the first; it is what experience has learned about the first object" (WW II, 70 [§86]).

First we must ask: What does the talk of "the new true object" mean? From the introductory sentence we can infer that experience is exercised on consciousness as a "dialectical movement." Consciousness is in itself the having-consciousness [*Bewußthaben*] of an object to which consciousness relates immediately. Insofar as one can speak of a "new true object" that arises from "consciousness" for the very first time, consciousness "has" properly speaking "two objects" in this experience. Hegel says: "We see that consciousness now has two objects: one is the first *in itself,* the second is the *being-for-it of this in itself"* (ibid. [§86]). Let us look at the example of consciousness in the shape of a sensible intuition, for instance the sensible intuition of this book here. The object of this sensible intuition (in the broad sense) is this book here, and it is intended in this sensible intuition as this sense object. This book here, which according to the opinion of sensible intuition is that which is in itself, *is*, however, "also" intuited, and therefore *as* something intuited at the same time it "is" "for it," namely for the intuitive consciousness. In the "in itself," as that which is indeed legitimately intended as such, lies nevertheless the "being-for-it-(consciousness)" of the in itself. This being-for-it is nothing else than the being-object [*Gegenstandsein*] of the object "book." The being-object and everything that belongs to it is called the objectness of this object. Objectness itself is not nothing but is only that which has until now continuously remained unknown to sense intuition. To the extent that the objectness of the object comes forth in addition to the usual and well-known object, it is something "new." If the objectness itself is specifically represented and intended, then *it* is "the new object." The being-object of the object (book) is determined by the being-for-consciousness of the book and thus appears to be nothing other than *the knowledge of the book* in the manner of the intuition of the book. But when considered up close, the objectness of the object is not something that is merely affixed to the object but that aside from this is of no concern to it. The first object (book) now rather becomes itself another; for *as* the object, it has now only come into that which it is, i.e., into its essence, namely into objectness. But the essence of something is what is "true" "in" an object. The objectness as the essence of the object is therefore not only "the new" object but at the same time and first and foremost "the true object." And according to the final sentence of the paragraph, this new true object contains "the nullity of the first." That is to say: The first object is "in itself" *not* that which is true, precisely because it is *only* "in itself," so that its objectness, i.e., its truth, does not yet come out. Viewed in this light, the first object (for instance, the book) is that which is un-true, that which is not-properly-true, that which viewed from its essence is that which is "null and naught." The new object—the objectness of the object—"is" its truth. But thus it "contains" that which the untrue object *as the untrue object* truly is; it contains its nullity. The new object "is" the experience concerning the first object.

What is that which one experiences in such an experience? It is something new and the true, namely the objectness of the object. The object of "the experience of consciousness" is the objectness.

And thus the first basic trait of Hegel's concept of experience, which supports all further moments, emerges in contrast to the Aristotelian and the Kantian conceptions. The ἐμπειρία is directed toward beings that are everywhere accessible in their everydayness. The Kantian "experience" is the mathematical natural science; as such it is directed toward the object "nature" that lies before us. However, it was Kant who for the first time in modern thought clearly carried out the inquiry into the being of beings and who developed this inquiry specifically into the shape of a question [*Fragestellung*] and outlined this question itself. For modern thought, a being is that which is represented to and placed alongside consciousness in consciousness for consciousness. Only now do beings become that which stands against [*Gegen-stand*] or objects [*Objekt*]. "Object" [*Gegenstand*] is the modern term for that which in actuality stands over and against [*Entgegenstehende*] the re-presentation that knows itself, the "object" [*Objekt*] for the subject. In modern thought, the actual, i.e., beings, is essentially object [*Gegenstand*]. In Greek thought, the concept of that which stands against [*Gegenstand*] and of the object [*Objekt*] is nowhere to be found because it is impossible here: man does not experience himself as "subject." Admittedly, Plato's theory of forms prepares the interpretation of the being of beings as objectness in a decisive manner. Since for Kant metaphysics does not inquire into beings but into being, which is very much in line with Greek philosophy, yet at the same time, following Descartes, the truth of being rests on the certainty of the representedness, the question of the being of beings, if understood in Kantian terms, is the question of the objectness of objects. This grasping of the objectness of the object is a completely distinct cognition, one that in relation to the immediate cognition of beings— nature—is a novel cognition. Kant therefore says: "I call all cognition transcendental that deals not so much *with objects but rather with our mode of cognition of objects insofar as this mode of cognition is to be possible a priori.* A system of such concepts would be called transcendental philosophy" (*Critique of Pure Reason,* "Introduction," B25 [149]). The cognition that deals with the objects themselves is for Kant experience. However, the cognition that thinks in the direction of the objectness of objects inquires into the conditions of the possibility of the object of experience. This grasping of the objectness of the object of experience in the Kantian sense is transcendental or ontological cognition. And exactly this letting-arise of the new true object in contrast to the old untrue one, this transcendental grasping of the objectness of objects, is what Hegel calls "experience." Thus, for Hegel "the experience" is *not* ontic cognition, as it is for Kant, but ontological cognition. This transcendental experience lets the objectness of the objects arise from "consciousness," it lets it emerge for the first time, namely in such a way that the objectness itself is now the object that has emerged for the first time and thus is the *new* object. This transcendental object is essentially, and not just incidentally, "the new" object. Its objectness consists in the "newness," in the having-emerged of the emerging through the experience. "Emerging" [*Ent-stehen*] does not mean:

being fabricated as a thing, but: to come to stand within and for representation, i.e., to appear. In Platonic terms: to become "viewable." But if according to Kant's fundamental step, which received its determination from Descartes, the conditions of the possibility of the object of experience lie "in consciousness," which means that they are nothing else than "self-consciousness," the essentially new object, i.e., the transcendental object, i.e., the object of Hegelian "experience," is nothing else than self-consciousness as such. But insofar as the latter constitutes the essence of consciousness, transcendental experience is essentially "experience of consciousness," and this in the threefold sense: Consciousness is that which is experienced in this experience, namely the objectness of the object. Consciousness is at the same time that which experiences, that which carries this experience out. And consciousness is therefore that to which what is experienced and the experiencing belong in such a way that consciousness itself "is" this experience.

Kant says: Transcendental cognition deals with the conditions of the possibility of experience (of the natural sciences), i.e., with objectness. Thus it is in line with Kant's thinking when we say that transcendental cognition as cognition also has its object, yet this object is not nature itself but consciousness. But why should the same question not be asked in relation to this transcendental object as well, i.e., the question about *its* objectness? Why should finite human consciousness itself, in which Kant finds the condition of the possibility of the object, and thus of objectness, not be interrogated about that through which it—self-consciousness—is *a priori* possible? Why should the transcendental question halt at the *first* new object—the objectness of the objects of the ontic cognition of mathematical natural science—and cease its inquiry here? Is this not only the very beginning of an inquiry from which, according to its essence, a new object must arise again and again, i.e., the conditions of the conditions of the possibility of the object of nature and so forth, all the way to the first all-conditioning unconditioned that is no longer itself conditioned?

These questions inquire "beyond" the question that Kant poses, albeit only in the way that was first opened by Kant himself. Indeed, we must still say more if we stay attentive to the traces of what is abyssal in Kant's thinking that can be encountered again and again, and if we do not want to degrade the *Critique of Pure Reason* to the status of a textbook. Kant understood consciousness as self-consciousness, but the self as "I"; and Kant sees in the essence of the I, i.e., in that it can say "I" to itself, the ground of this essence: reason. In a "Retraction" of his *Critique of Pure Reason*, Kant writes: "How it should be possible that I, who think, can be an object (of intuition) to myself, and thus distinguish myself from myself, is utterly impossible to explain, although it is an indubitable fact; it suggests, however, a power so far superior to all sensory intuition, that as ground of the possibility of an understanding . . . it looks out upon an infinity of self-made representations and concepts" (*What real progress has metaphysics made in Germany since the time of Leibniz and Wolff*, 362).[2]

Experience, as the transcendental letting-arise of the new true object, is necessarily related to an infinity, i.e., to consciousness as the in-finite, i.e., that which is not endless but what is originarily one, i.e., to consciousness as that which is *unconditioned* and all-conditioning. However, the relation of transcendental experience to what is unconditioned in consciousness is such that *this* "experience of consciousness" lets consciousness appear in its unconditioned truth and lets *consciousness show itself* in its complete conditionness that determines all objects in their possibility in a unified manner. Hegel's concept of "experience," in essential contrast to Kant's concept, is therefore not only in general ontological rather than ontic, i.e., transcendental in Kantian terms, but the experience that is in itself transcendental is directed toward what is unconditioned in all conditioning and thus toward the *entire* relation of conditioning. The "experience" is the unconditionally transcendental letting-arise of consciousness, the letting-appear of its shapes in the unconditionedness of their conditioning of all conditioned objects as such. Hegel and the metaphysics of German Idealism in general take this "looking out upon that infinity of self-made representations and concepts" seriously. To take this "looking out" seriously means not merely to add it here as a complement to Kant's transcendental inquiry and to view it alone as its end, but to begin with this looking out into the unconditioned and to let all "looking" be determined from here.

From this it becomes clear that Hegel uses the word "experience" as the name for unconditioned transcendental "cognition." This type of experience will therefore differ essentially from what is usually called experience. At the beginning of paragraph 15 Hegel explicitly refers to *one* of these differences in order to introduce, by way of this remark,

---

2. Kant, *Welches sind die wirklichen Fortschritte, die die Metaphysik seit Leibnizens und Wolffs Zeiten in Deutschland gemacht hat? (Preisschrift) Kant's gesammelte Schriften*, ed. Preußische Akademie der Wissenschaften, vol. 20, 270. Cf. ibid. in: Kant, *Zur Logik und Metaphysik. Dritte Abteilung: Die Schriften von 1790–93*, second edition, ed. Karl Vorländer (Leipzig, 1921), 95. [English: *Theoretical Philosophy after 1781*, trans. Henry Allison et al. (Cambridge: Cambridge University Press, 2010), 362; translation modified.]

the step toward that determination of the essence of "experience" that seeks to grasp its innermost core. The experience corrects (leads to the truth). Hegel says: "This exposition of the course of experience contains a moment in virtue of which it does not seem to agree with what is usually understood by experience. The transition, namely, from the first object and the knowledge of it to the other object *with which* one is said to have undergone the experience, was specified in such a way that the knowledge of the first object, that is, the being-*for*-consciousness of the first in-itself, is itself now supposed to become the second object. Whereas usually it seems to be the case that we undergo the experience of the untruth of our first concept *with another* object that we come across by chance and externally, so that our part in all this would be merely the pure *apprehension* of what is in and for itself" (Hoffmeister p.73 [§87]).[3]

What about the "usual" experience that we normally undergo? Ordinary experience is directed toward beings. We undergo our experiences of something with something. We thereby go from that of which we undergo the experience and with which we are in a way acquainted and which we take to be right and thus hold fast and initially "have," *over* to the other *with* which we undergo the experience. Experience is such a transition. We have for instance our representation of what a tree is, and we have taken this representation from the intuition of birches and beeches. On our course and during our journey through beings, an object steps in the way that is different from the birch and the beech. Our representation "tree" (e.g., with respect to the type of leaves that a tree can have) that we had until now is wrecked by this "other" object, namely the fir. The object that happens to come to us proves our old representation of a tree, i.e., the first object, to be inadequate, and that entails that it proves it to be an untrue object. We undergo the experience of the untruth of the first object with another object, namely in such a way that now we only have to look at the other object that is already present-at-hand—the fir—in order to correct our acquaintance with the tree by means of the experience. Insofar as the new experience is *not* undergone with the first object, the first object is not needed in the new experience. The experience remains directed toward objects, yet within the domain of this direction experience goes not toward the first but toward the other. Experience is thus the taking up of a finding that is dis-

---

3. Note from the German editor: From this point forward Heidegger cites the *Phenomenology of Spirit* after the edition by Johannes Hoffmeister: G. W. F. Hegel, *Phänomenologie des Geistes*, ed. J. Hoffmeister (Leipzig: Meiner, 1937).—The page numbers cited refer to this edition.

covered in another object that we come across, i.e., an object that is also already present-at-hand. In this experience it appears to us that our part is merely the pure apprehension and looking on; because we came across the other object in the same line of sight; it happened to come to us.

But what about the transition in the transcendental experience? It lets the objectness of the object come to sight and into view. What the first object is, i.e., what we experience about it as an object, its objectness, does *not* show itself here in *"another"* object but *precisely* in the *first one* itself, and only in the first. We do not let the first object go but we experience [er-*fahren*] *it*, we journey, as it were, *right through it*.[28] That which we experience, i.e., the experience that we undergo, shows itself in the first object in such a way that the object *itself becomes* another, i.e., it comes out in its objectness. This other object in which we now have a view of that which is to be experienced has emerged only as this other object that has come into being in this experience. In ordinary experience we go from the first object to another object that is already present-at-hand in the straight direction of ordinary consciousness away from something simply in order to apprehend this other object. In the transcendental experience, by contrast, we *stay* precisely with the *first* object of consciousness in such a way that what we are conscious of shows itself as that which a consciousness of it is conscious of [*das Bewußte eines Bewußtseins*]. The first object, not another object but the first itself, now shows itself, but in the direction of its standing-over-and-against to representation. In this direction in which the object stands over and against consciousness, the objectness of the object, i.e., the new other object, comes into "view." Therefore Hegel says regarding that which comes into view in the transcendental experience: "From that viewpoint, however, the new object shows itself to have come into being through a *reversal of consciousness* itself" (p.73f. [§87]). That is to say: 1. The objectness of the new object is the emergence. 2. The transcendental experience in which this emerging takes place is a self-reversal of consciousness. The transcendental experience in which the other new object is said to show itself is consequently not a pure apprehension and is no mere "looking on." The reversal of consciousness that prevails in the transcendental experience and that sustains it is a distinct way of looking at; and it is of such a "distinct" kind that Hegel must say the following about this kind of contemplation: "This way of contemplating the matter is our contribution, by means of which the series of the experiences of consciousness is raised into a scientific progression—but this contemplation does not exist for the consciousness that we are considering" (p.74 [§87]).

The "experience," i.e., the letting-itself-show of the object in its objectness, is therefore not a mere looking on and taking up but a "contribution." But now we recall that in the preceding paragraphs, which move toward the essential concept of experience and its demarcation at the beginning of paragraph 14, Hegel devotes all his efforts to showing that the presentation of appearing knowledge in its appearance must remain a "pure looking on." Hegel explicitly notes at the end of paragraph 12: "But the essential point to bear in mind throughout the whole investigation is that both of these moments, *concept and object, being-for-another* and *being-for-itself,* themselves fall within that knowledge which we are investigating, and that consequently we do not need to supply criteria and to apply *our* mere ideas and thoughts during the investigation; by leaving these aside, we succeed in contemplating the matter as it is *in* and *for itself*" (p.71f. [§84]). And directly after this, at the beginning of paragraph 13, he continues even more explicitly: "But not only is a contribution by us superfluous because concept and object, the criterion and what is to be examined, are present in consciousness itself, but we are also spared the trouble of comparing the two and of conducting a genuine *examination,* so that, while consciousness is examining itself, all that is left for us to do is simply to look on" (p.72 [§85]).

If, however, the transcendental reversal belongs to the essence of the experience of consciousness, and if this reversal is "our contribution," then the experience cannot be a "pure looking on." But have we already made sufficiently clear what in the domain in question something like the "pure looking on" is? Not at all. If we do not know yet what its essence is, it cannot simply be decided that "the pure looking on" excludes every contribution from itself. It could indeed be that the "pure looking on" demands the "contribution" in a pre-eminent sense and that without it it cannot be what it is. The essence of this "contribution" must be clarified, and we must see if and to what extent it belongs to the "pure looking on."

Our contribution is the "reversal of consciousness." By asking transcendentally, i.e., by making it our aim that the objectness of the object show itself, we turn the viewing direction of consciousness, which is normally directed toward objects, around and into the opposite direction, namely toward the *consciousness of* objects. The object that shows itself in this transcendental perception, namely the former object in the how of its objectness, i.e., objectness itself, is the object that thereby emerges for the first time and that is thus the new object. At the same time, however, in the decisive determination of the essence of experience Hegel calls this new, transcendental object the "true object." The truth of the object lies in what conditions its objectness in its essence and what constitutes this objectness. Yet we saw that Hegel's transcendental experience does not stop at self-consciousness as the condition of the objectness of the natural object, but that—following Fichte and Schelling's procedure—it also interrogates Kant's finite transcendental self-consciousness as the first new object about *its* objectness; it thus inquires into a connection of conditions and their conditioning that each time points beyond itself, all the way to the unconditioned. The newness of the new object and the truth of the true object consist in the *completeness* of its coming forth, i.e., of its emergence. This completeness of the appearance rests originarily in unconditioned, absolute self-consciousness. Absolute consciousness "is" the truth of the true object. Absolute consciousness, i.e., the consciousness that is essentially absolving, "is" the emergence, i.e., the newness of the new object, i.e., its constant appearance. The appearance is in fact the being-new. (A "new book" is "new" for us as one that appears to us and that is comprehended in its appearance.)

The manifold of these conditions is a unity that unfolds and is structured from the unconditioned. The manifold of these conditions that show themselves is irradiated and thus in advance and everywhere unified by that which shows itself, i.e., the idea that the absolute spirit itself is. Kant says at the end of the *Critique of Pure Reason* in the section on the architectonic of pure reason (A832, B860 [691] [29]): "By a system, however, I understand the unity of the manifold cognitions under one idea." According to this, the unity of the manifold of the transcendental conditions of the objectness of the object is a *systematic* unity. And *therefore,* in the section mentioned, which elucidates the essence of transcendental cognition, Kant immediately speaks of a "system of concepts." For Hegel's transcendental experience, the truth of the new object is absolute consciousness itself. Thus, insofar as the unity is a systematic unity it must be the unity of the absolute system. In the "Preface" to the *Phenomenology of Spirit* we read: "The true shape in which truth exists can only be the scientific system of that truth" (p.12 [§5]). The system, as the unconditionally certain connection of conditions in the unity of the unconditioned, posits within itself the manifold conditions into the order of a "series." By letting emerge the conditions of objectness, each of which is one condition more originary than the previous, experience—as the letting-arise of the new true object—opens up in advance the systematic realm of the *series* of experiences. Transcendental experience is as an unconditionally transcendental experience in itself systematic. And it is only from the full essence of the unconditioned-systematic transcendental experience that we can see what the nature of the "reversal of consciousness," which belongs to the essence of experience as a "contribution" by us, is.

The transcendental reversal of consciousness, to the extent that it is unconditioned and systematic, fixates in advance the view to what is unconditioned in all conditioning and its successive order. As that which conditions everything, the unconditioned stands in the fore-view for the letting-emerge of the new true object. But how does that which conditions, and it alone, come to light as such, i.e., in its conditionness? Only in such a way that what conditions shows itself in what is conditioned. If, however, not just any conditioning thing but the unconditioned itself is to appear in the manner in which it conditions everything, one must start from that which is the *most conditioned*. This, however, is *farthest away* from the unconditioned. Thus, the objectness of *that* object must show itself first that is farthest away from the truth of the unconditioned self-consciousness, i.e., from the non-sensible absolute spirit, and that stands at the extreme opposite end from it. Since the objectness of the most conditioned object is the condition that is the farthest away from the unconditioned, it can be only the emptiest and poorest objectness. However, to the extent that even the emptiest and poorest objectness of an object is still a condition, it is also from the essence of the absolute and belongs to it. To the extent that the transcendental turning is unconditioned and systematic, it is necessary that absolute consciousness distances itself from itself and its fullness and its rights in order to let its unconditioned conditioning appear in all that is conditioned. Absolute consciousness turns away from itself and toward its most external and most empty shape.

Absolute consciousness must externalize itself into its most external shape. Since consciousness, in turning *away from* itself in its fullness, turns yet again only to itself, albeit in its emptiness, the turning away is *only* a turning *around* in which absolute consciousness does not give itself up and does not leave itself. It is only in this turning around into the externalization that the expanse of a distance from itself opens up for consciousness. This open expanse of consciousness's own distance from itself within itself is as an expanse the free pathway for the journeying of experience. This open passageway is opened up only in the course of experience, i.e., it is explored [*er-gangen*] and experienced [*er-fahren*] on the journey. And it is only in this passageway that is opening up that absolute consciousness has the opportunity to return to itself. In this return to itself as the unconditioned truth, the latter, i.e., that which conditions unconditionally, comes to appear in its conditionness. The turn to externalization is necessary for the sake of the absolute, namely so that it has the opportunity to return to itself. *Because of that* the *Phenomenology of Spirit* begins with the presentation of the poorest and most untrue shape of consciousness, with "sense certainty," and ends with the shape of absolute self-knowing of spirit, i.e., absolute metaphysics. The *Phenomenology of Spirit* by no means begins with "sense certainty" out of pedagogical consideration for the human being, in order to initiate the course with the shape of consciousness that is the most likely to be understood by the human being. The first shape of consciousness in the *Phenomenology of Spirit*—sense certainty—is as far as our ability to understand is concerned in fact the most difficult one to understand, because in it the absolute must already be thought, albeit in its poverty and untruth (its not yet consummated truth). The course of the *Phenomenology of Spirit* is as it is not for our sake but for the sake of the absolute, and only for its sake. And how could it be otherwise if the cognition of the absolute is the ray by which the absolute touches us so that we think according to its will and not according to ours, provided that we think!

When we look closely at what Hegel calls the "reversal of consciousness," we see that it contains a double reversal: *on the one hand,* the turning of the object into its objectness that belongs to the essence of the transcendental in general; *on the other,* the turnabout into the externalization that is necessarily demanded by the unconditionedness and the systematics of absolute transcendental consciousness. This turnabout, as the turning away that is turned to the unconditioned, first opens up the course of the return. But according to Hegel's proposition, quoted earlier, this intrinsically twofold "reversal of consciousness," the transcendental turning and the absolute turnabout into the externalization, is "our contribution." *As* such it seems to disturb the "pure looking on," if not to destroy it. However, the opposite is the case. For it is only *when* the view upon the absolute and down the way of the return to it has been opened and paved by the double reversal that it is possible for the "new true object" to show itself on this open way. It is only this contribution [Zu-*tat*] of the reversal that gives the looking on the opportunity of a sight [*Sicht*] and a view [*Ansicht*]. But in other instances as well the "pure looking on" is never a mere passive receiving. Every looking-*on* is in itself a pursuit that goes along with; it is the casting of a glance that requires in advance a passageway that has been opened up. Moreover, the omission and non-application of our "mere ideas" is not nothing. The omission does not happen on its own. The ability to omit what is unsuitable is essentially determined by the constant prior involvement with the new true object and its unconditioned truth as the appearing criterion itself.

The purity of the pure looking on consists in no way of a divestment of all doing, but rather of the highest enactment of the deed that is an essential necessity for this looking and its possibility. That which this deed adds here is the looking ahead upon the unconditioned. The *look-*

ing ahead as a contribution to the *looking* on thus proves to be the pure taking-upon-oneself of that which is already contained in the looking on as its essential condition and which radiates toward us from the new true object as the ray, and which we are asked to expressly bring along as our own. Only the contribution [*Zu-tat*] that prevails in the reversal makes possible the pure looking on that is in accordance with its essence. This essence of the looking on, so conceived, is the essence of that "looking" (*speculari*) that is called "speculation" in the absolute metaphysics of consciousness. Speculative thinking lets consciousness show itself systematically in its transcendental unconditioned truth and thus is a "pointing out," taken in the strict sense that this word has in Hegel's language ("pointing out" = "not an immediate knowing"; cf. sense certainty, paragraph 19 [§107]). The pointing out is a prior laying open (the reversal) in such a way that in the open of this laying open the shapes of consciousness can "open up" in their objectness and show themselves for the first time. The pointing out is at the same time a showing-itself *and* a letting-arise (letting-emerge). Thus, the "pure looking on" as a transcendental pointing out in a way has the character of "activity" (laying open), at the same time, however, that of "passivity" (letting-itself-show and taking up). The originary unity of the representing faculty, which in its representations is both "active" [*activ*] and "passive" [*passiv*], reveals itself in what Kant and German Idealism call transcendental imagination. The "reversal of consciousness" is the essence of the "experience of consciousness." The experience is the transcendental-systematic pointing out that lets the "new true object" arise. This letting-arise pursues the object that is just emerging on the path of the return to itself. The objectness of this object is the emergence that shows itself in this pursuit. The emergence "is" and essentially occurs only in the emerging that is for the sake of pointing out, i.e., in and as experience. Experience is essentially a "course," i.e., a path on which and through which and in which the objectness of consciousness itself is explored [*ergangen*] and experienced [*erfahren*]. The experience that one "undergoes" on this course is not lost; for by being essentially correcting, i.e., by leading to the true object, the experience, as this essential correction, is the objectness of the true object. As a course, this path is the movement of the coming into being of the objectness of the object. But the latter is consciousness itself, and its objectness is its emerging into the truth of its essence. The path is consciousness itself as the emergence of its truth. The objectness of the object is the "formal aspect" [*das Formelle*] in the strict sense of that which determines. (Cf. for instance Kant's distinction of nature in a "formal" and a "material" respect. Form means the "existence [*Dasein*] of things" as the being of beings. The material aspect concerns the scope of beings themselves.) The "formal aspect" is not the outer nondescript form but the essentially occurring essence [*wesende Wesen*] of consciousness to the extent that it is in itself the self-appearance in whose appearance it manifests its objectness. Experience as the transcendental-systematic course into the truth of consciousness is as pointing out at the same time the presentation of appearing knowledge. As a transcendental systematics this presentation is in itself "scientific," i.e., it is commensurate with the essence of the absolute knowledge that knows itself. Because of this, after the decisive remark about the "reversal of consciousness," Hegel immediately says the following about this reversal: "This way of contemplating the matter is our contribution, by means of which the series of the experiences of consciousness is raised into a scientific progression—but this contemplation does not exist for the consciousness that we are considering" (p.74 [§87]). According to the essence of experience, which is determined by the reversal of consciousness, the difference between that which is "for us" and that which is "for it," i.e., for consciousness, necessarily and constantly obtains in experience.

This distinction between the "for us" and the "for it" constantly recurs on the course of the entire work. The "for us" is the object for the transcendental-systematic experiencers who look toward the objectness of the object, i.e., upon the emergence of its emerging. "For us" does *not* mean" "us" who just live along in our everydayness and who momentarily come to appearing knowledge, but *us* who look on in the manner of the reversal. "For it," however, means consciousness that freely unfolds its shapes historically as self-consciousness and that preserves these shapes in the memory of historiology, and thus knows itself in the fullness of its content. Both that which is "for it," i.e., for consciousness, and that which is "for us" do not coincide with what we usually think of as the domain of objects. Rather, each time this distinction concerns absolute spirit: in the "for it" it concerns absolute spirit in its history, and in the "for us" it concerns absolute spirit in the historicity of the history of its appearance. The historicity is the developed systematic, i.e., the organization of the labor of the concept. (Cf. the final sentence of the entire work.)

That which in the experience of consciousness is "for us," the essential truth of its objectness, shows itself only by virtue of the reversal. In this reversal we take the object not according to that which draws us to it in terms of its content, so that in going toward it we take it from the front. In the reversal of consciousness, i.e., in looking at the objectness of the object we do not go toward the object but we go around it and take it, as it were, from behind. But the objectness that the reversing experience aims at is consciousness itself. Hegel therefore says of the emerging of the new object that it "proceeds, as it were, behind its {namely consciousness's} back" (ibid. [§87]). For consciousness, i.e., "for it," everything that emerges in it is only as that which has emerged itself. The object that has emerged is "for us" as the "new true object," i.e., in its emerging, i.e., the object "at the same time as movement and a process of becoming" (ibid. [§87]). But this emerging in its emergence is the essence and the truth of consciousness. As this essence, this emerging is thus at the same time a *necessary* stepping forth, a necessity of consciousness itself, if its truth is indeed the unconditioned certainty of itself in the completeness of what is to be known in its essence.

Now the sentences that conclude paragraph 15 and that, at same time, constitute a segue to a short transitional section that, in turn, forms a bridge to paragraph 16—the fifth part—become more intelligible:

"However, it is just this necessity itself, or the *emerging* of the new object, which presents itself to consciousness without consciousness knowing what is happening to it, which proceeds for us, as it were, behind the back of consciousness. Thus in the movement of consciousness there occurs a moment of *being-in-itself* or *being-for-us* that does not present itself to the consciousness that is comprehended in the experience itself; the *content,* however, of what we see emerging exists *for it,* and we comprehend only the formal aspect of it, or its pure emergence; *for it,* what has emerged exists only as an object, whereas *for us* it exists at the same time as a movement and a process of becoming" (ibid. [§87]).

From this it becomes clear that the transcendental systematic presentation is not offered to the experience of consciousness as an addition, but that the experience itself as the letting-arise of the "new true object" is a pointing out and thus a presentation [*Dar-stellung*]. This presentation pursues the return of the conditions into the conditioning of the unconditioned and is thus a course that receives its necessity from the essence of the objectness of the new object. This yields the following sentence, in which Hegel summarizes the discussion of the "Introduction" up to this point in order to express the interpretation of the title of the work: "Because of this necessity, this path to science is itself already *science,* and in terms of its content is thus the science of the *experience of consciousness*" (ibid. [§88]).

In other words *and* looking back to the beginning of the "Introduction" this means: The "experience of consciousness" is the course that belongs to its essence and that leads to it as self-consciousness. Since the cognition of the absolute is essentially a course, and that means a path, the examination that examines absolute cognition can take this "cognition" never as a "means," nor as a "tool" that is at our disposal nor as a present-at-hand "medium." This presentation of appearing knowledge as the unconditioned transcendental-systematic science is that toward which the experience of consciousness unfolds: its suitable ether. The appearance of this science does not succumb to the semblance of arbitrarily entering the scene, as if shot from a pistol, in an indeterminate domain. The appearance of science is the self-presentation of experience, which—out of its essence, namely out of the reversal—opens up the domain of the appearance of consciousness for the latter, but at the same time necessarily determines the beginning of the course, the progress of the course, and before all the goal of the course of appearance. (Cf. "Preface" about "experience," p.32 [§36].) In the return of the absolute consciousness from the externalization to itself, which is a return that is itself already transcendentally oriented, the appearance of the unconditioned is carried out. Consciousness appears, i.e., it steps out of itself and into "view" by going back into itself. It manifests itself by entering into its concept (λόγος) which it is for itself. Consciousness is φαινόμενον, that which appears, as λογία in the mode of such a science. Consciousness *is* consciousness as "phenomenology." Since, however, consciousness is *appearing* knowledge, yet absolute self-knowing is *spirit*, the phenomenology is essentially "the phenomenology *of* spirit." Since consciousness turns itself forth in the return, the course of its appearance is essentially a "reversal." If the reversal is our "contribution" to the "looking on," then this contribution [*Zu-tat*] "adds" nothing foreign to consciousness. The contribution only brings the looking on to the enactment of its innermost essence. The contribution is the first and highest act of the looking on, which thus in advance sees to it, i.e., looks and watches out to ensure, that the absolute is respected as the absolute and thus only the absolute and not something else comes to appearance.[30] The "experience of consciousness" is the "phenomenology of spirit." The "experience," however, is only as the experience that presents itself, i.e., as science. The *Science of the Experience of Consciousness* is the *Science of the Phenomenology of Spirit*.

Only now are we in the position to become aware of the concealed content of these two titles. At first and if taken thoughtlessly, the title *Science of the Experience of Consciousness* denotes for us a science "of the" experience, the experience that is undergone "concerning" consciousness. We think the two genitives as *genitivus objectivus* and grasp the title by fixing its semantic content in the first word, "science." But if we now remember the elucidation of the "Introduction" that was given, we know that consciousness itself demands and carries out the "experience" of its own accord, namely in such a way that the experience that is carried out has to present itself necessarily as science. We must therefore understand the title from its last word and in the opposite direction. This "reversal" signifies at the same time that the genitives must not be thought as *genitivus objectivus* but as *genitivus subjectivus*. Consciousness is the subject, that which supports the experience; the latter is the subject of science. However, since the word "consciousness" is the "subject" not only in a grammatical logical sense but also according to its metaphysical essential content, the *genitivus subjectivus* here is a *genitivus subjectivus* in an "emphatic sense"; for consciousness is essentially "subject" in the meaning of "self-consciousness"; yet the essence of the latter consists in that by knowing its other, i.e., the object, it knows itself at the same time. With respect to the subjectivity that is named essentially in the title by the word "consciousness," the *genitivus subjectivus* can accordingly not be a *genitivus subjectivus* in the usual sense; since the subject remains at all times related to an object, it is at the same time also a *genitivus objectivus*. Therefore, the title must be thought in such a way that the genitives are primarily, i.e., determinatively, understood as *genitivus subjectivus,* which implies, however, that they are at the same time understood as *genitivus objectivus*. And yet, we would still not hit the core of the truth of the title if we thought that the genitives would have to be thought as both "subjective" and "objective." The decisive thing is to recognize that neither the "thetic" interpretation of the title (in the sense of *gen. obj.*), which is the most obvious one, nor the "antithetic" one (in the sense of *gen. subj.*) is sufficient. The genitive that must be thought here is the "synthetic" one, which does not push the two aforementioned genitives together after the fact, but thinks the ground of their unity originarily. This ground of their unity is the essence of the "experience" itself in which appearing knowledge, consciousness, appears to itself in its appearance as "science." The "genitive" that is to be thought here is the originarily synthetic one, i.e., the "dialectical-speculative" genitive that the language of this work employs everywhere.

Strictly speaking, language has no "grammatical" forms for these relations of the essence of consciousness, and that means for the actuality of the actual of modern metaphysics. Language, which according to Hegel always immediately "expresses" the universal and thus speaks it away from itself, is therefore unable to say what is to be thought in the opposite direction of all of spirit's externalization, i.e., what is to be thought with respect to its return to itself. Language must therefore disappear in relation to "consciousness itself" if the latter is to be thought truthfully, just like it fades away as expression in the utterance of the sound. Hegel says at one point in his *Jena Lectures,* crucial portions of which prepare the elaboration of the *Phenomenology of Spirit:* "Language must fade away in consciousness, just like it fades away in the air."[4]

We therefore understand the first, determinative utterance of the *Phenomenology of Spirit,* i.e., its first chosen title—*Science of the Experience of Consciousness*—, which is interpreted in the "Introduction," only when the wording and the understanding that is at first suggested by it has truly disappeared into knowledge. This disappearance, however, must be enacted in a letting-disappear. This happens in the "experience" that no interpretation of the "genitives," whether taken by themselves or together, is sufficient in order to grasp what is essential here. But *because* the matter of the language of thoughtful thinking stands like this, this language is not left to arbitrariness but is bound into a stringency, and all mere measuring to the objects of description and recounting falls infinitely short of this stringency.

But why did Hegel let the title *Science of the Experience of Consciousness* disappear? Was the word "experience" for him, after all, too charged in the direction of the non-speculative, i.e., "empirical" usage? And yet, the words "experience" and "experiencing" constantly recur in the work on the course of the *Phenomenology of Spirit*—namely in the sense that they receive in the "Introduction"—and it is furthermore printed in italics in the preface (Hoffmeister p.32 [§36]) that was written *after* the introduction. (The immediate as what is not experienced.) Therefore, this word and what it means cannot be contrary to spirit itself and its "phenomenology." And indeed it is not contrary to it. For what is "spirit"? Hegel concludes his second and definitive system, the "Encyclopaedia-system," not with his own words but with a Greek text whose words are taken from Book Λ of Aristotle's *Metaphysics* (ch.7). In these sentences the beginning of Western metaphysics, whose consummation Hegel considered his own work to be, speaks. In these sentences Hegel lets the spirit of Western metaphysics itself say, from its beginning, what spirit is. Spirit is νοῦς. And in the section quoted by Hegel Aristotle says of the "actuality" of the νοῦς: ἡ γὰρ νοῦ ἐνέργεια ζωή (Λ 7, 1072 b 27), "The pure being-at-work out of itself, i.e., the presencing of the apprehension of the presence of everything that is present, is life." Translated into modern terms: "The actuality of spirit is life."

---

4. G. W. F. Hegel, *Jenenser Realphilosophie I,* ed. Johannes Hoffmeister (Leipzig, 1932), *Hegels Philosophie des Geistes von 1803–04.* Cf. 235.

Cf. also *Jenenser Philosophie des Geistes,* in *Jenenser Realphilosophie II* (1931), 183. [English: *System of Ethical Life and First Philosophy of Spirit,* trans. T. M. Knox and H. S. Harris (Albany: SUNY Press, 1979), 226; translation modified.]

2. Guiding propositions to Hegel's concept of experience

We now know: Consciousness is the appearing spirit and thus "life" in its appearance to itself. But if "experience" is determined from the essence of consciousness, its essence arises from the essence "of life." "Experience" is a part of life. To live "life" means nothing else than to be experienced in the experience of life. If we ponder these connections, then it can no longer appear strange that in Hegel's concept of "experience" the concealed and scattered essential elements of "experience" come to light, precisely because the concept of "experience" is taken in the transcendental sense and thus denotes the non-empirical speculative experience of spirit. We will try to name the essential moments that come to appearance in Hegel's concept of experience in the form of short guiding propositions:

1. Experience is *pervagari*—a journeying traversal of courses.[31]

2. This traversing experience does not stick to rutted paths; in the process of journeying through courses it opens the courses to passageways for the first time.

3. The traversing-opening experience is experience in the originary sense of πεῖρα. This means the involvement with something with the intention of seeing what comes out of it, i.e., what appears. The involvement with . . . , as it were, the "taking on" of the opponent for a competition, brings each time a decision one way or another. Experience is the confrontation [*Auseinandersetzung*] with something; it is "dialectical" insofar as the setting-asunder [*Aus*einander*setzung*] essentially sets what is set asunder [Aus-*einander-Gesetzte*] into the light, i.e., lets it appear.

4. As this involvement with something that lets appear, experience sets that which results from it (i.e., the new) in relation to what came before. Experience is a weighing, probing, and examining. The ἐμπειρία is the journeying and going and standing in the πεῖρα, the looking on that gets involved with and examines.

5. But since the involvement goes through a decision every time, in each instance the experience is in some respect a correction; and thus the decision that is contained in the experience proves to be the notification about what is right and what is not right, about what is true and what is untrue. Since the experience is correction, it lets a new true object arise each time.

6. Experiences do not take place on their own. It is always *we* who undergo experiences in the manner of a proceeding [*Vorgehen*] and undertaking [*Vornehmen*]. Experience itself steps expressly into its realm, and as such an event [*Veranstaltung*] it is not a coincidental tak-

ing cognizance but an *experiri,* an *experimentum.* Where the proceeding of experience assumes the character of a self-empowered attack on the appearances, experience begets the "experiment" in the modern sense of a technical intervention. By getting involved with something, experience each time also "takes a chance" on what it undertakes.[32] Experience is not only a weighing and examining but at the same time a venturing.

7. In venturing and getting involved experience intervenes into that which appears, namely in such a way that this intervention produces precisely that which appears in its appearance. The intervening and seizing production that places itself in the service of the appearance is the essence of labor. The experience is essentially labor. Insofar as the experience is the experience of consciousness and the latter is for itself its own concept, the concept itself has to be "labor." Hegel therefore speaks multiple times of the "labor of the concept." By this he does not mean the corporeal-psychic effort and strenuousness of thinking but the essential manner of the proceeding in comprehension according to which comprehension takes up the deed [*Tat*] of the contribution [*Zutat*] and stands in the service of the "reversal."

8. The labor-character of experience does not exclude but indeed implies the fact that all experience and undergoing of experiences contains a "going through" in the sense of a suffering and enduring. Experience endures the violence of that wherein it is raised [*erhoben*] and with which it is in each case involved. The wealth of experience is determined by the strength to suffer.

9. At one with this moment of "going through," the experience is "painful." The pain of the experience is not a consequence of it as a kind of impact on our corporeal-psychic state. The pain is rather the innermost essence of the experience in which all previously mentioned moments have their unity and determinateness. The pain is essentially consciousness and knowledge. The pain is the essence of knowing insofar as the latter is constantly a passage through the corrections that each experience contains. Every experience is, essentially understood, a dis-illusionment. It lets what was hitherto held fast come out as that which is untenable. The so-called good experience that we undergo with something is a dis-illusionment as well. In such cases we are "pleasantly" dis-illusioned. But if that is the case, is it still true that every experience is "painful"? Indeed, *every* experience is a pain, pain in the sense of the consciousness of the transposedness into the necessity of going through the dis-illusionment as the only path of the truth of consciousness to itself. Since consciousness is self-consciousness, it is never the indifferent differentiation of itself from itself, but in this differentiated being-itself it is only equal

to itself as the being-other to the other. This manifold united differentiatedness of consciousness in itself, the being-itself in the manner of the absolute being-other, is the essential ground of the tearing that appears at every stage of consciousness so long as it is not absolute in an absolute sense. By turning around toward externalization and then back from it, experience goes through the tearing of consciousness; since experience is the knowledge of this tearing, it is this pain itself. (On tearing, pain, and the labor of negativity, cf. "Preface" p.29 [§32], especially p.20 [§19] about the essence of the absolute— "Pain" cf. also the end of *Faith and Knowledge,* p.190.[33]—experience as boldness—mindful courage.)

Every experience as experience is painful, because as experience it is a "bad experience," i.e., one in which the badness (not the moral wickedness) of the violence of the negative manifests itself. Even the seemingly "good" and "pleasant" experience is, essentially understood, a "bad" one.

That is the abyssal essence of experience. If Hegel indeed understood the appearance of consciousness as a course of the essential disillusionment, he must have encountered this essence of experience that is the essence of life itself.

In comparison to this fulfilled concept of experience, the empirical concept of experience of the empirical and of the empiricists is only the insipid and dried-up sediment of a formerly lively drink.

But Hegel still let the title *Science of the Experience of Consciousness* disappear. Was the full essence of "experience" not sufficiently present to him in its unity and for that reason does not figure as the guiding word of the title? Why was the title dropped?

We do not know.

It is enough that it has remained preserved for us as the strange impetus for a reflection that thereby sees itself pushed into a confrontation with absolute metaphysics and thus becomes prepared for the pain of the diremption from it.

V. ABSOLUTE METAPHYSICS
(SKETCHES FOR PARAGRAPH 16
OF THE "INTRODUCTION")

1. Essential considerations. Objectness and "science"

The *Phenomenology of Spirit* is the *conceptual history* of the appearing absolute, the history of spirit "from { . . . } its conceptual organization" (cf. the final sentence of the work)—i.e., its systematics—the system. This *standing-together* in a single consciousness that *is* unconditioned self-consciousness and that consists in this standing-together for itself.

The "forms" of the system are not compartments that are forced onto consciousness ("empty organization"—that does not exist), but these forms are themselves the concealed essential shapes of consciousness, i.e., its objectness for it itself (the new true object).

And in this *objectness* it is precisely not the form *of* consciousness that comes out but *consciousness itself* in its innermost essence as "form"—as "I think."

The form of the organization and *negativity.* The negation of negation.

The decision lies deeply concealed here: that "consciousness" and object and objectness at all occur essentially in the primacy of the absolute.

Truth as certainty. Being as idea and category. *Being* as objectness and "idea."—Being and thinking.

2. At a glance 1

"The sense certainty itself" "is" "only this history of its experience."

Its truth, i.e., its certainty, i.e., the self-certainty of consciousness that is commensurate with it, consists in the "movement" (μεταβολή) of the letting-arise of the new true object ("Introduction," paragraph 14 [§87]).

("Movement" is here re-presentingly representing, i.e., a representing change-over (ἐχ—εἰς) of representation as a placing-*toward-oneself*.—"Movement" not "change in location.")

Object 1. the new object, 2. the true object.

Experience—not with "another" object but with the same, namely in such a way that in the experience this object turns out to be another.

The truth of sense certainty as the truth of immediate knowing is *mediation*.

The objectness of the new true object is *mediatedness* (negation of the negation).

The objectness (unconditionally transcendental) is "negativity." What is the relation between "*negativity*" itself and the *objectness* that was first determined by Kant:

objectness and "reflection"	negativity and "negation"
"thinking"	"thinking"

Objectness and certainty. Certainty and "science." "Science" and its justification: as the letting-appear of its concept. Science and the system.

3. The ray of the absolute. At a glance 2

The "system" and the "object"—(the "obtaining-together"), "Transcendental Deduction" §16.

The "*Phenomenology of Spirit*" and the *Logic* (cf. *Logic* 1812, p.X [28]).[1]

"Introduction"—Examination of cognition.—Cognition as "tool and means."—Cognition as "path," as course, as "*movement.*"

Now explicitly: Cognition as the "*movement* of experience." The latter, however, is as certainty—itself the "truth" of the absolute. The path is the truth itself—the appearing true thing in its appearance [*Erscheinen*] and manifestation [*Scheinen*]. This manifestation is the radiating of the absolute itself. The ray that touches "us"—us who inquire in a transcendental unconditioned manner, i.e., *the ones who look-on*—in the "contribution" [*Zu-tat*] of the view toward the new true object.

The "deed" is only the enactment of what has already happened.

---

1. For this edition cf. above p.51, footnote 4.—In Georg Lasson's edition (Leipzig, 1923) volume I, 29.

4. The phenomenology of spirit

Hegel—Descartes (objectness and truth in their unity).

Cf. *Phenomenology,* "Introduction," final paragraph and the *Logic* 1812, "Introduction," p.Xf. [28].[2] Here Hegel says: "In the *Phenomenology of Spirit* {note the shortened title} (Bamberg and Würzburg 1807) I have presented consciousness as it progresses from the first immediate opposition of itself and the object to absolute knowledge. This path runs through all the forms of the *relation of consciousness to the object* and its result is the *concept of science.* This concept, therefore, requires no justification here (apart from the fact that it emerges within logic itself), because it has already received one in said place; and it is not capable of any other justification other than its production by consciousness, all of whose shapes dissolve into the same {the concept} as into their truth."

Here it becomes clear that in the transcendental transformation, *despite* all that is left over of the shapes of spirit, indeed *as a result* of it, Descartes's inquiry is with all the more reason and properly consummated. "Science" = the knowledge of absolute knowledge: the unconditioned certainty as actuality itself. This actuality, however, is the *objectness* of unconditioned thinking (I think).

5. The movement

The clarification of the concept "movement" important

1. from μεταβολή
2. with regard to re-presentation, looking on-contribution, reversal [*Um-kehrung*]
3. with the inclusion of sub-lation
4. with regard to cognition as "path," spirit—course
5. as determination of "becoming"

6. The by-play [Bei-her-spielen]

Singularization in the *essence* of *intuition: single things represented immediately,* (a) from the *object,* (b) out of the mode of *releasing.*

The particularization essentially in all consciousness—out of the "reflection" and the appearance.

---

2. Ibid. [*Science of Logic,* 28.]

* * *

Kant's supreme principle of all synthetic judgments and Hegel's formula from the preface to the *Philosophy of Right* each say in their own manner that being is actuality—objectness, that truth is—certainty. [34]

7. The examination

"The examination"—of experience—the unconditioned transcendental reversal.

Hegel does not deny the precedence of an *examination* of absolute cognition before the consummate absolute cognition of the absolute. But its essence is of a different type, *namely* the letting-oneself-be-touched by the ray—to follow the ray.

Thus conversely: To pursue the ray while being hit and guided by it. *The reversal.*

8. The onto-theological character

Wherein the onto-theological character of metaphysics is grounded (the ray). Like a descent from the τὸ γὰϱ αὐτὸ νοεῖν ἐστίν τε καὶ εἶναι.[35]

* * *

The absolute metaphysics of German Idealism not a hasty transcending of limits but the seriousness of taking seriously what has been assigned. Not *hasty* but the highest thoughtfulness that above all and decisively keeps thought in all that exists here (the unconditioned).

Beyng-historical thinking, from which alone the essence of metaphysics lights up, is thoughtful in yet a completely different manner.

9. The reversal

The thinker (man) is touched by the ray, and out of this touch and only in accordance with it he can think the absolute.

The thinker thinks from himself toward the absolute, and his cognition presents itself in *that* shape.

But this cognition is conversely the radiating of truth upon the thinker.

Thus, in order to cognize truthfully he must follow this radiating.

Thus, he must carry out a reversal—; and to what extent does he thus conform to what the absolute itself must demand in order to show itself in its course?

10. The Germans and metaphysics

For the Germans the historical moment may come in which they would have to become attentive to that which awaits them as their own. That which is their own can only be appropriated in the essential confrontation that lets the essential become question-worthy. To this day, the German relation to the metaphysics of German Idealism remains entangled in an either-or whose historical grounds can be passed over here. Either blind rejection = rejection without understanding of absolute metaphysics or an equally blind parroting, and that in the bad form of its adaptation to the requirements of the times.

Getting bogged down in this either-or contains the danger of a ruinous downfall.

11. The absolute and man

The absolute is not pulled into cognition in toil and pain. Cf. Schelling VII, 135.[3]

Not to *give* anything but to take away what is contingent [*Zu-fällige*]. The remainder—the essence of man himself.

What is this essence? And from where and how is it to be determined? *How* is man and is he ever *in* his essence or even just on the way to it? From where and which characteristics?

12. Reflection—counter push—reversal

The "reversal of consciousness" our contribution through which the *series* of appearances is reversed.

The *series* is not *for* the consciousness that we are considering but "for us."

---

3. F. W. J. Schelling, *Sämmtliche Werke*, ed. K. F. A. Schelling (Stuttgart and Augsburg, 1856–61). [Heidegger is referring to a passage from the "Vorrede" to the *Jahrbücher der Medicin als Wissenschaft*, which Schelling edited from 1806 to 1808 together with A. F. Marcus.]

But *who* we? Those who think philosophically. Philosophy—nothing outside of us and nothing that comes on the scene.

The *reversal* of the *series of appearances* ("the entire series of the essential shapes of consciousness"[36]); these experiences are not "made"[37] by us but taken up—but in the reversal.

But this reversal as well demanded by experience as transcendental, i.e., *necessary* from the essence of *reflection.*

Only this *necessary* reversal—its necessity itself is the *"for us."*

But properly speaking not purely "through" *us.*

13. Projection and reversal

The philosopher does not first give himself a relation to the absolute but forgets *himself* in this relation that already is. The self-forgetting, however, his contribution—and not nothing.

Self-forgetting, i.e., the letting-prevail of the ray. *Being radiated upon, to be* a *ray,*—this ray, however, the *lighting up that shows itself.*

To go alongside this ray toward oneself, the thinker. Thus, to be outside oneself and to come to and to bring to oneself.

Outside oneself—in the *projection.* To project *what?* That which *appears*—"object." *How, in terms of what?* Its *objectness.*

To exhibit the what—to add the how. But the *how* only in the mode of and following its appearance.

14. Experiences as transcendental experiences

The possibility and necessity of the experiences of consciousness lie in the latter itself as "reflection" in which the absolute *wills* to reveal itself in its truth. This will its—actuality.

This "reflection" is the casting back of its own light into itself and thus the *showing-itself*—the *radiating. The ray* is reflection.

Our cognition—a "reversal" that is demanded by the "reflection" itself.

The "experience" is movement, is the *becoming conscious* of the essence of the experiencing spirit, is *philosophy* itself as the *history* of the experience of the essence of the absolute.

This experience is the *objectness* of the standing-against of spirit, the *having-appeared of appearance itself.*

The voluntary of the will—the actuality of what is true.[38]

"Consciousness itself" is "comprehended" in this experience and is "the content." *That which is experienced is for it.*

Which unconditioned knowledge (presentation) does the experience of consciousness thereby demand for itself—the *experience* of consciousness.

15. The metaphysics of Schelling and Hegel

The metaphysics of Schelling and Hegel as the return to Leibniz, shaped {?} and essentially clarified by Kant's transcendental philosophy, namely in such a way that Leibniz's metaphysics is now understood metaphysically in the transcendental-ontic sense.

16. "Phenomenology" and absoluteness

Conclusion: cf. paragraph 13.

Question: What does the disappearance of the *Phenomenology of Spirit* from the determinative role in the system signify?

If the system is the absolute itself,—the absolute *in that form* not yet in its *consummate completion*! This absoluteness, however, becomes decisive because the forgetting of being has become consummate in *absolute* certainty! Everything achieved, i.e., nothing anymore.

Relation [*Bezug*] to "man." In *what* sense? (Cf. with respect to Schelling, anthropomorphism). The absolute essence of the relation [*Relation*].

Man and being.

17. Confrontation with Hegel

1. Consciousness, therefore
2. The transcendental—being as objectness, the old untrue object—actuality as idea.
3. Truth as certainty.
4. Man as subject—self-consciousness.
5. The being that is most in being—the absolute; subjectivity as unconditioned subject-object.
6. The system and the organization of history. Absolute metaphysics and technology.
7. The new true object, i.e., beingness as consciousness-of-beings [*Bewußtseiendheit*] is the object of representation. Placing-before-oneself [*Vor-sich-stellen*]—knowing will—being as will. The absolute *wills* to be with us.
8. Negativity and the truth of beings as being.

18. Hegel (Conclusion)

Absolute metaphysics, unconditioned speculation and *"experience."*

Experience (cf. *Encyclopedia* §7/8) the *principle* of modernity. The being-alongside of man; not just "also" alongside but the essential instance of the demonstration—before the insight—evidence. Cf. §37ff. "Empiricism."

Subjectivity. Absolute metaphysics as modern metaphysics. *Experience* not "positivism" and blind sensibility and "fact" but in the essential sense of *certainty.*

Man—*anthropomorphism cf. Schelling.*

Man and "beings."

APPENDIX

Supplements to I–IV (paragraphs 1–15 of the "Introduction")

1. Dialectic

Dialectic (cf. as an example "Sense certainty," paragraph 20 [§109]) as the name for the *objectness* (i.e., truth) of *consciousness* in its appearance, *the being-spoken-through that expresses itself,* λόγος—διά. *Platonic*-transcendental, not Kant's transcendental dialectic.

2. Our contribution [*Zu-tat*] (cf. p.90ff.).

Our contribution [*Zu-tat*] is the explicit enactment of the looking on, namely of the supporting and guiding and opening *looking-out upon . . .* , the *explicit enactment* of the transcendental *I unite, I connect* that occurs essentially in consciousness itself.

The transcendental, however, is in itself intended as a reversal—*re-flection* (in itself already). The re- not *in addition to* but already concealed in the *re-praesentare*.

3. The reversal—properly speaking four essential moments

as *turning*—the transcendental
as turn *into* the externalization
as *return* from the externalization into the *transcendentally* viewed *unconditionedness*
as *return* the *turning forth* of the transcendental

4. The experience as the essential midpoint of consciousness

"The experience" not as procedure but as the essential midpoint of consciousness: it is the "reflection" in and as "movement," life, spirit.

"The experience" that consciousness undergoes with itself is the *transition* from the "for it" to the "for us" and back again; but this back finds another object. (The "we" in the "for us" "are" the essence of consciousness in its transcendental truth.)

The dis-illusionment—the disappearance.

The "transition"—the constant going through of this back and forth as movement "is" what is essential.

This movement, however, is not one manner of proceeding among others but is the proper essence of consciousness, which is ontic-ontological in itself.

Therefore only a first step: the step toward consciousness as self-consciousness. The second and proper step is: to *comprehend* the "I think" as transcendental. *The return to self-consciousness* as the *transcendental turning.*

And the transcendental turning as the concealed truth and the ground of every return of consciousness to itself in its contingent history.

Editor's Afterword

These two treatises were grouped together by Martin Heidegger for a separate Hegel-volume for the *Gesamtausgabe*. The two treatises belong together both in terms of the time of their composition and in terms of their content. Although the texts are at times fragmentary and some passages in either text contain addresses to an audience, which indicates that they were composed for an oral presentation, Heidegger explicitly assigned them as *treatises* to the third division of the *Gesamtausgabe*.

The treatise on "Negativity" from 1938/39 consists of notes strung together in pieces that allow for a continuous reconstruction. The drafts are worked out to different degrees and in different ways. They range from detailed parts in which the rhythm of the speaker can still be discerned, to "glances" with a clearly numbered outline of thoughts, to "sketches of thought," as I would like to call them, that is, they are brief unfoldings of a concept or simply different approaches of the inquiry and what are at times tentative answers. As such, these notes offer formidable insight into the workshop of Heidegger's way of thinking, questioning, and elucidating.

The treatise that seeks to elucidate the "Introduction" of Hegel's *Phenomenology of Spirit* from 1942 offers a different picture. What we have here is a continuous text that divides the sixteen paragraphs of Hegel's "Introduction" into five parts and that—after a preliminary consideration—interprets these paragraphs in a way that follows the text for the most part. Only the final part, titled "Absolute metaphysics," was not worked out. Instead it consists of drafts of thoughts of the kind described above.

Although the fact that the texts were composed for an oral presentation cannot be missed, it remains unclear at least for the text on "Negativity" what the occasion for the composition was and for what audience Heidegger undertook it. In fact it is unclear whether the text was ever presented *in this form* at all. The documents detailing Heidegger's seminars (course catalogues, Heidegger's own lists, seminar registers) give no indication. In the winter semester of 1938–39 Heidegger did not teach a graduate seminar but only a beginner's seminar on a text by Nietzsche.

The notes on "Negativity" may have been presented to a small circle of colleagues, the so-called philosophical *Kränzchen*.[39] Evidently the audience that Heidegger addresses here is one that was to a degree familiar with Hegel's philosophy and that occupied themselves with Hegel's *Logic.*

Perhaps a presentation before this circle of colleagues was also the occasion for the "Elucidation of the 'Introduction' of Hegel's *Phenomenology of Spirit.*" We find some evidence for this in *Off the Beaten Track,* which Heidegger himself published in 1950. This work also contains an elucidation of the introduction to the *Phenomenology of Spirit,* titled "Hegel's Concept of Experience." However, this elucidation has a completely different style. In the "List of Sources" Heidegger writes, "The contents of the essay were thoroughly discussed in a more didactic form in seminars on Hegel's *Phenomenology of Spirit* and Aristotle's *Metaphysics* (Books IV and IX) 1942–3, and during the same period presented in two lectures before a smaller audience" (GA 5, p.375).[40]

Both manuscripts, like many others too, were transcribed by Fritz Heidegger. In the winter of 1941–42 Heidegger undertook the transcription of "Negativity," presumably for the purposes mentioned above. He also added handwritten supplements. They are for the most part abbreviated references. They have been supplemented with bibliographical information and are printed here in the footnotes. Due to what seems to have been an accident, three full pages of the manuscript of the "Elucidation of the 'Introduction' of Hegel's *Phenomenology of Spirit*" were put in the supplements, which had the effect that Fritz Heidegger did not transcribe them as was the case with the other supplements. The pages in question are the chapter "The Experience [*Erfahrung*] of Consciousness," which fits well at the end of part three and in all likelihood was written for it.

For the publication both manuscripts were carefully read, or deciphered, and compared to the transcriptions as far as these were available. Omissions were supplemented, reading errors were corrected, and later additions were incorporated as footnotes.

The structure is indicated in both manuscripts. The individual paragraphs in each of the five parts of "Negativity" were numbered consecutively. In the odd case where subheadings were missing they were added (in the form of a keyword that matches the content of the paragraph). The same was done for the supplements.

Following *Contributions to Philosophy* (GA65), the publication of this book marks the publication of a second volume from the third division. In contrast to the lectures of the second division, where in accordance with the wish of the author small imperfections of the oral presentation had to be compensated for the sake of a carefully constructed text, the texts of the third division follow the handwritten original copy more closely. For the many sketches of thought this means that every underlining and every quotation mark was preserved even if this leads to doubled emphases. The abundance of underlining and quotation marks is characteristic of the author's style of work.

Most of the citations come from Heidegger himself. The necessary bibliographical additions are based on the copies used by Heidegger from his own library and from the Philosophical Seminar of the University of Freiburg. In a few cases quotations were completed.

*   *   *

I would like to cordially thank Dr. Hermann Heidegger, Prof. Dr. Friedrich-Wilhelm v. Herrmann, and Dr. Hartmut Tietjen for always having been kind and willing to help with questions of deciphering, problems of organization, and the search for sources, as well as for their critical review. I would also like to thank Prof. Dr. Klaus Jacobi and cand. phil. Mark Michalski for their help with the citations of quotations that were hard to locate.

Stuttgart, June 1993.   Ingrid Schüßler

Translators' Notes

[1.] "Das erste, 'Was' wird, ist das *Werden* selbst."

[2.] "Mindlessly" translated the German *rücksichtslos*, which literally means "without hindsight" or "without looking back."

[3.] "Ahead" translated the German *Voraus*. Heidegger says that the *Vor* in *Voraussetzung* must be understood as the *Voraus*. The English translation of *Voraussetzung* as "presupposition" does not allow for the same kind of morphological-semantic distinction.

[4.] The expression *zu Grunde gehen* normally means "to perish" or "to founder." However, when taken literally it means "to go to the ground."

[5.] "In the beginning was the Word" (John 1:1).

[6.] "Object-of-consciousness" translates the German *ein Bewußtes*. Heidegger frequently uses the term *das Bewußte* to refer to the object or content of consciousness. We have translated *das Bewußte* for the most part as "the object-of-consciousness." The hyphenation is meant to indicate that Heidegger is not speaking of the *Gegenstand* of consciousness. In cases where Heidegger mentions *das Bewußte* in the same sentence in which he also speaks of "the object of consciousness" [*Gegenstand des Bewußtseins*] we have translated the former as "that which consciousness is conscious of."

[7.] Heidegger contrasts the *Ein-* of *Einfall* with the less intrusive *an-* of *angefallen*: "Wenn der Einfall *nicht Ein*fall,—wenn das Ganze als solches *an*gefallen in seinem ihm ungefragten und unfragbaren Grunde."

[8.] "Soul, spirit or mind, reason."

[9.] Heidegger translates *nobis consciis*—"we being conscious"—as *die wir* uns mit*wissen*, which in English may be rendered as "we who *also* know *ourselves*" or "we who know *ourselves along with*." He translates *conscientia* according to the meaning of its constituent elements *cum* (*mit*/with) and *scientia* (*Wissenschaft*/knowing) as *Mitwissenschaft*, which we chose to translate as "accompanying knowing."

[10.] The second part of Heidegger's quotation does not appear in the German edition in this form. It is thus a paraphrase rather than a direct quotation. The German text of Hegel's *Phänomenologie des Geistes* reads, "wenn es nicht an und für sich schon bei uns wäre und sein wollte."

[11.] As Heidegger explains on p.78, the word *Gang* must be understood in the double sense of "the process of going"(or "a going" [*das Gehen*]) and "passageway" (or "path"). We have chosen to render *Gang* consistently as "course."

[12.] "Absolving" translated the German *Absolvieren*, which is the nominalization of the verb *absolvieren*. It means "to complete," "to pass," "to finish successfully," "to work through." Heidegger says that *Absolvieren* is a *Vollbringen*, that is, an "accomplishment" or an "achieving." (Cf. also p.79.) *Absolvieren* also names the process in which a person is given an absolution, that is, the process in which a person is pronounced free from guilt. Heidegger unites these two meanings of *absolvieren* in the term *Absolvenz*, which we have rendered as "absolvence." "Absolvence" is at the same time a successful completion and the (resulting) absolution.

[13.] There is no mention of "violence" at WW II, 60 [§73]. Even though the German edition of *Hegel* makes no mention of this, it appears that the phrase "the (absolute) violence" is Heidegger's own.

[14.] Translation modified.

[15.] "Das Bewußtsein verhält sich als solches zu seinem Bewußten (dem 'Gegenstand'), und indem es diesen auf *sich* als *es selbst* bezieht, verhält es auch schon *sich zu sich* selbst."

[16.] In German, the two preceding sentences read as follows: "Es ist einmal streitendes, prüfendes Sichauseinanderlegen, Streitgespräch mit sich selbst. Als dieses Auseinanderlegen ist es und legt es sich heraus und aus und ist das Sichdarlegen in der Einheit des in sich Gesammelten."

[17.] Heidegger hyphenates the German *Er-fahren* here. Unlike the English "ex-" in "experience," the *Er-* in *Erfahren* emphasizes the doing or making involved in experience. *Fahren* can mean to drive, ride, go, and navigate, and so in hyphenating this word, Heidegger is emphasizing how this is an undertaking that we must take. One could render this as "go or take the path" as well.

[18.] *Gang*, which throughout this volume we have translated by "course," is a noun derived from *gehen* ("to go"). In German the sentence reads, "Der Weg ist ein Gang in dem zwiefachen Sinne des Gehens (Gang aufs Land) und des Durchgangs (unterirdischer Gang)." Despite the contrast that Heidegger creates between the activity of going and the object of a passage, the word *Durchgang* ("passageway") is itself employed in the double sense of "a passageway" (*Durchgang* as an object) and a passing through (*Durchgang* as a process). While Heidegger notes the ambiguity of *Gang* early on (cf. our translators' note on p.65), he does not make explicit that this ambiguity also applies to those compound nouns that have *Gang* as their constituent component. To highlight this difference we use "passageway" and "passage" to translate *Durchgang*.

[19.] "Diese bedeutet das Sicheinlassen auf etwas aus dem Absehen auf das, was dabei herauskommt."

[20.] At this point we have deviated from our general rule of translating *Bewußtsein* by "consciousness." Although Heidegger does not hyphenate *Bewußtsein* here, the meaning of the sentence is obscured unless *Bewußtsein* is rendered as "being-conscious."

[21.] The verb *abarbeiten* can also mean "to complete a given list of tasks." Both meanings of the word *abarbeiten* resonate here.

[22.] "Movement from something into something. Actuality." See Aristotle, *Physics,* 225a1.

[23.] "All human beings by nature desire to know." See Aristotle, *Metaphysics,* 980a22.

[24.] "Alle Menschen haben die aus dem Grund ihres Wesens aufgehende Vor-liebe (alles, wozu sie sich verhalten) sich zu Gesicht zu bringen, um es in seinem Aussehen anwesend zu haben (εἰδέναι—ἰδεῖν)."

[25.] "To be familiar" is our translation for *Kunde haben.*

[26.] Translation modified.

[27.] In current editions these words are printed in italics.

[28.] "Wir lassen hier den ersten Gegenstand nicht fahren, sondern *er*-fahren *ihn,* fahren *durch ihn* gleichsam hindurch."

[29.] Translation modified.

[30.] "Die Zutat ist der erste und höchste Akt des Zu-sehens, das so im vorhinein zusieht, d.h. darauf sieht und achtet, daß das Absolute als das Absolute geachtet wird und so nur das Absolute und nicht irgend etwas anderes zum Erscheinen kommt." Heidegger here exploits the dual meaning of *zusehen: zusehen* with the direct object means "to look on something"; *zusehen* followed by a that-clause means "to see/watch out to ensure that something happens."

[31.] "Die Erfahrung ist pervagari—ein hindurchfahrendes Durchmessen von Gängen."

[32.] In German this sentence reads, "Indem das Erfahren sich auf etwas einläßt, läßt es auch das Vorgenommene jeweils 'auf etwas ankommen.'" The expression "es auf etwas ankommen lassen" pertains to the moment of risk in πεῖρα.

[33.] G. W. F. Hegel, *Faith and Knowledge,* trans. Walter Cerf and H. S. Harris (Albany: SUNY Press, 1977). In the passage in question Cerf and Harris translate *Schmerz* as "grief."

[34.] Heidegger is again referring to "What is rational is actual; and what is actual is rational." See Hegel, *Philosophy of Right,* 20.

[35.] "For thinking and being are the same." See G. S. Kirk, et al., *The Presocratic Philosophers: A Critical History with a Selection of Texts* (Cambridge: Cambridge University Press, 1983), 269.

[36.] *Phenomenology,* §87.

[37.] At this point we have deviated from our general idiomatic translation of *eine Erfahrung machen* as "to undergo an experience" in favor of the more literal "to make an experience" in order to preserve the contrast in the German original between *machen*, "make," i.e., a productive activity, and *aufnehmen*, "take up."

[38.] "Das Willentliche des Willens—die Wirklichkeit des Wahren."

[39.] The *Kränzchen* ("small circle") was a small gathering that took place on a regular basis.

[40.] Translation taken from *Off the Beaten Track*, 285; translation modified.

German-English Glossary

Abbau, der	dismantling
Abfall, der	decline
Abgrund, der	abyss
abgründig	abyssal
Abkehr, die	turning away
Absage, die	renunciation
Absolvenz, die	absolvence
Absolvieren, das	absolving
abwenden	to turn away
alltäglich zugänglich	accessible in its everydayness
Andersheit, die	otherness
Anderssein, das	being-other
anfallen	to tackle
Anfang, der	beginning
Annehmen, das	taking on
Anschauung, die	intuition
Ansich, das	in itself
Ansicht, die	view
Anweisung, die	indication; directive
Anwesenheit, die	presence
Anwesung, die	presencing
Arbeit, die	labor
Auffassen, das	apprehension
Auffassung, die	conception
auffinden	to discover, come across
Aufgabe, die	giving up
Aufheben, das	sublation, preservation
Aufhellung, die	illumination
aufleuchten	to light up
Auflösung, die	dissolution
Aufnehmen, das	taking up
Aufschließen, das	laying open
Aufsichnehmen, das	taking-upon-oneself
Aufsteigerung, die	elevation
Aufstockung, die	augmentation
Auftreten, das	coming on the scene
aufweisen	to exhibit
Aufzeigen, das	pointing out
Ausarbeitung, die	elaboration
auseinanderlegen	to explicate; to lay asunder
Auseinandersetzung, die	confrontation
Auseinandertrag, der	carrying-part

auseinander tragen	to carry apart
Ausführung, die	realization
Ausgang, der	emergence; point of departure
ausgehen	to emerge, proceed
Ausgleich, der	conciliation
ausgleichen	to compensate
Auslegung, die	interpretation
aussagen	to assert
Außerachtlassung, die	disregard
Aussetzung, die	suspension
ausüben	to exercise
Ausweisung, die	demonstration
Auswirkung, die	impact
Bahn, die	way
Bedachtsamkeit, die	thoughtfulness
Bedenken, das	pondering
Bedenken, die	concerns
bedenklich	thought-provoking
Bedingen, das	conditioning
Bedingnis, die	conditioning; conditionness
bedürfen	to require
befragen	to interrogate
Beginn, der	inception
begreifen	to comprehend, conceive
Begriff, der	concept
Begründung, die	grounding
Bei-sich-selbst-sein, das	being-with-oneself
Berichtigung, die	correction
beschließen	to resolve (upon)
Besinnung, die	meditation, mindfulness
Besonderung, die	particularization
Bestimmtheit, die	determinateness
Bestimmung, die	determination
Betrachtung, die	consideration; contemplation
beugen	to bend
Bewegung, die	movement
Bewußte, das	object-of-consciousness
Bewußt-sein, das	being-conscious, being an object of consciousness
Bewußtsein, das	consciousness
beziehen	to relate, refer
Beziehung, die	relation, relationship
Bezug, der	relation
Blick, der	view, gaze
Blickrichtung, die	viewing direction, line of sight
Dabei-sein, das	being-alongside
Darlegung, die	exposition

darstellen	to present
Darstellung, die	presentation
denkerisch	of thought, thoughtful
Drehung, die	turning
durcharbeiten	to work through
Durcharbeitung, die	elaboration
Durchgang, der	passageway; passage
durchlaufen	to traverse
Durchmachen, das	going through
Durchmessen, das	traversal
durchmessen	to traverse
eigentlich	proper
eigentümlich	peculiar
Einbezug, der	implication
Einfall, der	mere idea, intrusion
einfallen	to intrude (on)
eingreifen	to intervene
Einheit, die	unity
einholen	to catch up to
einigen	to unite
einkehren	to enter
Einräumung, die	making room (for)
Einsicht, die	insight
Einsprung, der	leap into
Einzigkeit, die	singularity
Elevation, die	elevation
Empirische, das	empirical (evidence)
Entäußerung, die	externalization
Entfaltung, die	unfolding
Entfernung, die	distancing
Entgegensetzung, die	contraposition
Entgegenstehen, das	standing over and against
entgültig	definitive
Entscheidung, die	decision
Entscheidungsnot, die	need for decision
Entschiedenheit, die	resoluteness
entspringen	to arise
Entspringenlassen, das	letting-arise
Entständnis, das	emergence
entstehen	to emerge, come into being
Entstehen, das	emerging
Entstehenlassen, das	letting-emerge
Enttäuschung, die	disillusionment
Entwerden, das	expulsion from becoming
Entwerfen, das	projection
Entwurf, der	projection; sketch
Entzweiung, die	diremption

Ereignis, das	event
Ereignung, die	eventing
erfahren	to experience
Erfahren, das	experience
Erfahrung, die	experience
Erfahrung machen	to undergo an experience
erfassen	to grasp
erfragen	to inquire (into)
ergehen	to explore
erheben	to raise
Erkennen, das	cognition
Erkenntnis, das/die	cognition
erklären	to explain
erlangen	to attain
Erläuterung, die	elucidation
Erleiden, das	suffering
Erleuchten, das	lighting up
Ernst machen (mit)	to take seriously
eröffnen	to open up
erörtern	to discuss
Erörterung, die	discussion, exploration
Erscheinen, das	appearance
erscheinende Wissen, das	appearing knowledge
Erscheinenlassen, das	letting-appear
ersehen	to bring into view
Erspringung, die	leaping attainment
erstehen	to stand forth
Erstreckung, die	expanse
Fahren, das	journeying
Fahrt, die	journey
fassen	to grasp
Fassung, die	conception
Frage, die	question
Fragebereich, der	realm of inquiry
Fragen, das	inquiry
fraglich	questionable
Fraglosigkeit, die	questionlessness
fragwürdig	questionworthy
Für-das-Bewußtsein-sein	being-for-consciousness
Für-es-sein	being-for-it
Gang, der	course
Gedachtheit, die	thoughtness
Gefüge, das	framework, structure
Gegensatz, der	opposition
Gegenstand, der	object; what stands against
Gegenständliche, das	objective
Gegenständlichkeit, die	objectness

Gegenstandsein, das	being-object
Gegenwart, die	present
gemeines Denken	common thought
Gesamtheit, die	totality
geschehen	to happen
Geschehnis, das	happening
Geschichte, die	history
geschichtlich	historical
Geschichtlichkeit, die	historicity
Gesicht, das	sight
Gesichtskreis, der	horizon
Gestalt, die	shape, form
gleichursprünglich	co-originary
Grund-	basic-
gründen	to ground
Grundgefüge, das	basic structure
Grundsatz, der	basic proposition
grundsätzlich	fundamental
Grundstellung, die	basic position
Gründung, die	grounding
Grundverfassung, die	basic constitution
Grundverhältnis, das	basic relation
Grundwort, das	basic word
Grundzug, der	basic trait
herabsetzen	to degrade
Herausgerissenwerden, das	being-wrested
Herausstellen, das	exposition
Herrschaft, die	rule
Hervorkommen, das	coming forth
Hervortreten, das	stepping forth
herzubringen	to supply
hinaufheben	to raise up
hinaufsetzen	to raise
hinausdenken	to think in the direction
hinausgehen (über)	to transcend
hinaussehen (auf)	to look out (upon)
Hinblick, der	regard
Hinsehen, das	looking at
Hinsicht, die	regard
Hinweis, der	indication; directive
hinzubringen	to supply
Historie, die	historiology
historisch	historiological
innestehen	to stand in
Inständigkeit, die	insistence
Im-Gesicht-Haben, das	having-in-sight
Kenntnis, die	acquaintance (with things)

Kenntnisnahme, die	cognizance
kennzeichnen	to characterize, determine
Klärung, die	clarification
Kunde, die	familiarity, information
Kundnahme, die	taking notice
Langweiligkeit, die	boringness
Leitfaden, der	guiding thread
Leitsatz, der	guiding proposition
Lichtung, die	clearing
Loslassen, das	release
Loslösung, die	detachment
Lossprechung, die	release
Machenschaft, die	machination
Mangel, der	lack, deficit
Mannigfaltigkeit, die	manifold
maßgebend	determinative
Maßstab, der	criterion
Mensch, der	man, human being
Menschwesen, das	human being
Mitwissen, das	co-knowing
mitwissen	to know also/alongside
Mitwissenschaft, die	accompanying-knowing
Nachdenken, das	reflective thinking
nachgehen	to pursue
Nachtrag, der	supplement
Negieren, das	negating
Neuheit, die	newness
Nicht, das	the not
nichten	to nihilate
nichthaft	not-like
Nichtheit, die	not-ness
nichtig	null and naught
Nichtige, das	what is null and naught
Nichtigkeit, die	nullity
Nichtsein, das	not-being
Nichtung, die	nihilation
Not, die	need, distress
Objekt, das	object
Objektivität, die	objectivity
offenbaren	to reveal
Ort, der	location
Prinzip, das	principle
Prinzipsein, das	being-principle
Prüfung, die	examination
Reflexion, die	reflection
Reihe, die	series
Rückblick, der	review

Rückgang, der	regress
Rückkehr, die	return
Sachverhalt, der	matter
Sammlung, die	gathering
Schaffen, das	creation
Scheiden, das	separation
Schein, der	semblance
Scheinen, das	manifestation, shining
Schritt, der	step
Schutz, der	shelter
Seiende, das	beings
Seiende an sich, das	beings in general
Seiende im Ganzen, das	totality of beings
Seiendheit, die	beingness
Seiendste, das	the being that is most in being
Selbigkeit, die	self-sameness
Selbstbesinnung, die	meditation on oneself
Selbstentäußerung, die	self-externalization
Selbsterscheinen, das	self-appearance
Selbstsein, das	being-itself
Selbstsicherung, die	self-assurance
Selbstverständlichkeit, die	self-evidence
Seyn, das	beyng
sich aufhalten	to tarry, linger
sich ausweisen	to prove itself, demonstrate
sich entäußern	to divest oneself; to externalize
sich erweisen	to prove (to be)
sich herausstellen	to prove itself
sich loslassen	to release itself
sich verhalten	to comport itself
sich vordrängen	to push itself to the front
sich wissen	to know itself
Sich-auf-sich-selbst-beziehen, das	relating-itself-to-itself
Sichauseinanderlegen, das	laying-itself-asunder
Sichaussprechen, das	self-expression
Sichdarlegen, das	self-exposition
Sichdarstellen, das	self-presentation
Sich-denken, das	thinking-itself
Sicheinlassen, das	involvement
Sicherhalten, das	self-preservation
Sichoffenbaren, das	self-revelation
Sichselbstbegreifen, das	self-comprehension
Sichselbsterscheinen, das	appearing to itself
Sichselbstwissen, das	knowing itself as a self
Sicht, die	sight
Sichunterscheiden, das	self-differentiation
Sichvergessen, das	self-forgetting

Sichwissen, das	self-knowledge, knowing itself
Sichzeigen, das	showing-itself
Sichzeigenlassen, das	letting-itself-show
Sich-zu-stellen, das	placing-toward-oneself
sinnliche Anschauung, die	sense intuition
sinnliche Gegenstand, der	sense object
Sprung, der	leap
stiften	to found
Stimmung, die	attunement, mood
Strahl, der	ray
strahlen	to radiate
Streitgespräch, das	disputation
Stufe, die	stage
Stütze, die	support
Subjekt, das	subject
Synthesis, die	synthesis
System, das	system
Systematik, die	systematics, system
Systemteil, der	part of the system
tragen	to support
tragend	underlying, fundamental
Trennung, die	division
Übergang, der	transition
Übergehen, das	passing-over
Übergriff, der	encroachment
Überlegung, die	deliberation, consideration
Überlieferung, die	transmission
übersteigen	to transcend
Überwindung, die	overcoming
Umkehrung, die	reversal
Umschlagen, das	change-over
Umwendung, die	turning around, turnabout
Unbedingtheit, die	unconditionedness
Unbegriff, der	non-concept
unbedingt	unconditioned, unconditionally
unbestimmt	undetermined, indeterminate
Unbestimmtheit, die	indeterminateness, indeterminacy
Unentschiedenheit, die	undecidedness
Unmittelbarkeit, die	immediacy
unterscheiden	to differentiate
Unterscheidung, die	distinction, differentiation
Unterschiedenheit, die	differentiatedness
Ur-sache, die	originary cause
Ursprung, der	origin
ursprünglich	originary
Vereinzelung, die	singularization
Verhältnis, das	relationship, relation

Vergegenwärtigung, die	making-present
Vermitteltheit, die	mediatedness
Vermittelung, die	mediation
Vermögen, das	faculty
Vernehmen, das	apprehension
Verneintheit, die	negatedness
Verneinung, die	negation
Vernichtung, die	annihilation
Vernommenheit, die	perceivedness
Versagung, die	refusal
Verschiedenheit, die	distinctness
Verschwindenlassen, das	letting-disappear
Versetztheit, die	transposedness
Verstand, der	understanding, intellect
Verstehenkönnen, das	ability to understand
Verwahrlosung, die	neglect
Verweigerung, die	refusal
verweilen	to tarry
verwirklichen	to actualize
Vollbringen, das	accomplishment
Vollendung, die	consummation
Vollständigkeit, die	completeness, totality
vollziehen	to carry out
Vollzug, der	to enactment
Vollzugsform, die	form of enactment
Voraufgehen, das	precedence
voraufgehend	previous, prior
Voraus-habe, die	pre-possession
Voraus-nahme, die	anti-cipation
Voraussehen, das	looking ahead
Voraussetzung, die	presupposition
vorauswerfen	to throw ahead
Vor-blick, der	fore-view
Vordenken, das	fore-thinking
vorfinden	to come across, discover
Vorgabe, die	pregiven(ness)
Vorgang, der	process
Vorgehen, das	approach, procedure
Vorgestelltheit, die	representedness
Vorhabe, die	fore-having
Vorhaben, das	undertaking
vorhanden	present-at-hand
Vorrang, der	primacy
Vor-sich-haben, das	having-before-oneself
Vor-sich-stellen, das	placing-before-oneself
Vorstellen, das	representation; placing-before
Vorstellung, die	representation

wagen	to venture
wägen	to weigh
wahrhaft Seiende, das	what truly is a being
wahrhaft	truly, truthfully
Wahrnehmung, die	perception
walten	to prevail
Wandel, der	transformation
Wechselbeziehung, die	interrelation
Wechselbezug, der	correlation
Weg, der	path
Wendung, die	turning
wesen	to occur essentially
Wesensauszeichnung, die	essential characteristic
Wesensbau, der	essential structure
Wesensbesitz, der	essential property
Wesensbestand, der	essential structure
Wesensbestimmung, die	essential determination
Wesensentfernung, die	essential distancing
Wesenserfahrung, die	experience of the essence
Wesensfestsetzung, die	essential definition
Wesensgehalt, der	essential content
Wesensmitte, die	essential midpoint
Wesentlichkeit, die	essentiality
Wesung, die	essential occurrence
Wettkampf, der	competition
wirken	to have an impact, be effective
Wirklichkeit, die	actuality; actual relevance
wirksam	effective
Wirkung, die	impact, effect(s)
Wissen, das	knowing, knowledge
Zerrissenheit, die	tearing
uns zufallen	to happen to come to us
zufällig	contingent, coincidental
Zugewiesenheit, die	allotment
Zugehörigkeit	belongingness
zugrunde gehen	to run aground; to go to the ground
zugrunde legen	to lay down
zugrunde richten	to wreck
Zulassung, die	permission
zum Vorschein kommen	to come to light
zur Erscheinung bringen	to make manifest, bring to appearance
Zur-Kenntnis-nehmen, das	taking cognizance
Zusammenfallen, das	coinciding, coincidence
Zusammengehörigkeit, die	belonging-together
Zusammenhang, der	connection, relation

Zusammensehen, das	synopsis
Zusammensetzung, die	composition
Zusammenstehen, das	standing together
zuschaffenmachen	to tackle
Zusehen, das	looking on
Zu-sich-selbst-kommen, das	coming-to-itself
Zuständlichkeit, die	states
Zutat, die	contribution

English-German Glossary

ability to understand	Verstehenkönnen, das
absolvence	Absolvenz, die
absolving	Absolvieren, das
abyss	Abgrund, der
abyssal	abgründig
accompanying-knowing	Mitwissenschaft, die
accomplishment	Vollbringen, das
acquaintance	Kenntnis, die
actuality	Wirklichkeit, die
to actualize	verwirklichen
actual relevance	Wirklichkeit, die
allotment	Zugewiesenheit, die
annihilation	Vernichtung, die
anti-cipation	Voraus-nahme, die
appearance	Erscheinen, das
appearing knowledge	erscheinende Wissen, das
appearing to itself	Sichselbsterscheinen, das
apprehension	Auffassen, das; Vernehmen, das
approach	Vorgehen, das
to arise	entspringen
to assert	aussagen
to attain	erlangen
attunement	Stimmung, die
augmentation	Aufstockung, die
basic-	Grund-
basic constitution	Grundverfassung, die
basic position	Grundstellung, die
basic proposition	Grundsatz, der
basic relation	Grundverhältnis, das
basic structure	Grundgefüge, das
basic trait	Grundzug, der
basic word	Grundwort, das
beginning	Anfang, der
being an object of consciousness	Bewußt-sein, das
being-conscious	Bewußt-sein, das
being-itself	Selbstsein, das
beingness	Seiendheit, die
being-object	Gegenstandsein, das
being-other	Anderssein, das
being-principle	Prinzipsein, das
beings	Seiende, das

beings in general	Seiende an sich, das
the being that is most in being	Seiendste, das
being-with-oneself	Bei-sich-selbst-sein, das
being-wrested	Herausgerissenwerden, das
belongingness	Zugehörigkeit, die
belonging-together	Zusammengehörigkeit, die
to bend	beugen
beyng	Seyn, das
boringness	Langweiligkeit, die
to bring to appearance	zur Erscheinung bringen
to bring into view	ersehen
to carry apart	auseinander tragen
carrying-apart	Auseinandertrag, der
to carry out	vollziehen; ausführen
to catch up to	einholen
change-over	Umschlagen, das
to characterize	kennzeichnen
clarification	Klärung, die
clearing	Lichtung, die
cognition	Erkennen, das; Erkenntnis, das/die
cognizance	Kenntnisnahme, die
coinciding, coincidence	Zusammenfallen, das
co-knowing	Mitwissen, das
to come across	vorfinden
to come into being	entstehen
to come to light	zum Vorschein kommen
coming forth	Hervorkommen, das
coming on the scene	Auftreten, das
coming-to-itself	Zu-sich-selbst-kommen, das
common thought	gemeine Denken, das
to compensate	ausgleichen
competition	Wettkampf, der
completeness	Vollständigkeit, die
to comport itself	sich verhalten
composition	Zusammensetzung, die
to comprehend, conceive	begreifen
concept	Begriff, der
conception	Auffassung, die; Fassung, die
concerns	Bedenken, die
conciliation	Ausgleich, der
conditioning	Bedingnis, die; Bedingen, das
conditioneness	Bedingnis, die
confrontation	Auseinandersetzung, die
connection	Zusammenhang, der
consciousness	Bewußtsein, das
consideration	Betrachtung, die; Überlegung, die
consummation	Vollendung, die

contemplation	Betrachtung, die
contingent, coincidental	zufällig
contraposition	Entgegensetzung, die
contribution	Zutat, die
co-originary	gleichursprünglich
correction	Berichtigung, die
correlation	Wechselbezug, der
course	Gang, der
creation	Schaffen, das
criterion	Maßstab, der
decision	Entscheidung, die
decline	Abfall, der
deficit	Mangel, der
definitive	entgültig
to degrade	herabsetzen
deliberation	Überlegung, die
to demonstrate	(sich) ausweisen
demonstration	Ausweisung, die
detachment	Loslösung, die
determinateness	Bestimmtheit, die
determination	Bestimmung, die
determinative	maßgebend
to differentiate	unterscheiden
differentiation	Unterscheidung, die
differentiatedness	Unterschiedenheit, die
directive	Anweisung, die; Hinweis, der
diremption	Entzweiung, die
to discover	auffinden
to discuss	erörtern
discussion	Erörterung, die
disillusionment	Enttäuschung, die
dismantling	Abbau, der
disputation	Streitgespräch, das
disregard	Außerachtlassung, die
dissolution	Auflösung, die
distancing	Entfernung, die
distinction	Unterscheidung, die
distinctness	Verschiedenheit, die
distress	Not, die
to divest oneself	sich entäußern
division	Trennung, die
effect(s)	Wirkung, die
(to be) effective	wirksam; wirken
elaboration	Ausarbeitung, die; Durcharbeitung, die
elevation	[in Part I] Aufsteigerung, die; [in Part II] Elevation, die

elucidation	Erläuterung, die
to emerge	entstehen; ausgehen
emergence	Entständnis, das; Ausgang, der
emerging	Entstehen, das
empirical (evidence)	Empirische, das
enactment	Vollzug, der
encroachment	Übergriff, der
to enter	einkehren
essential characteristic	Wesensauszeichnung, die
essential content	Wesensgehalt, der
essential definition	Wesensfestsetzung, die
essential determination	Wesensbestimmung, die
essential distancing	Wesensentfernung, die
essential midpoint	Wesensmitte, die
essential occurrence	Wesung, die
essential structure	Wesensbau, der; Wesensbestand, der
essentiality	Wesentlichkeit, die
event	Ereignis, das
eventing	Ereignung, die
examination	Prüfung, die
to exercise	ausüben
to exhibit	aufweisen
expanse	Erstreckung, die
experience	Erfahren, das; Erfahrung, die
to experience	erfahren
experience of the essence	Wesenserfahrung, die
to explain	erklären
to explicate	auseinanderlegen
exploration	Erörterung, die
explore	ergehen, to
exposition	Darlegung, die; Herausstellen, das
expulsion from becoming	Entwerden
externalization	Entäußerung, die
to externalize	sich entäußern
faculty	Vermögen, das
familiarity	Kunde, die
fore-having	Vorhabe, die
fore-thinking	Vordenken, das
fore-view	Vor-blick, der
form	Gestalt, die
form of enactment	Vollzugsform, die
to found	stiften
framework	Gefüge, das
fundamental	grundsätzlich; tragend
gathering	Sammlung, die
gaze	Blick, der
to go through	durchmachen

to go to the ground	zugrunde gehen
to grasp	fassen, erfassen
to ground	gründen
grounding	Begründung, die; Gründung, die
guiding proposition	Leitsatz, der
guiding thread	Leitfaden, der
to happen	geschehen
to happen to come to us	uns zufallen
happening	Geschehnis, das
to have an impact	wirken
having-before-oneself	Vor-sich-haben, das
historical	geschichtlich
historicity	Geschichtlichkeit, die
historiological	historisch
historiology	Historie, die
history	Geschichte, die
horizon	Gesichtskreis, der
human being	Mensch, der; Menschwesen, das
illumination	Aufhellung, die
immediacy	Unmittelbarkeit, die
impact	Auswirkung, die
impact	Wirkung, die
implication	Einbezug, der
inception	Beginn, der
indeterminacy	Unbestimmtheit, die
indeterminate	unbestimmt
indeterminateness	Unbestimmtheit, die
indication	Anweisung; Hinweis
to inquire (into)	erfragen
inquiry	Fragen, das
insight	Einsicht, die
insistence	Inständigkeit, die
intellect	Verstand, der
interpretation	Auslegung, die
interrelation	Wechselbeziehung, die
to interrogate	befragen
to intervene	eingreifen
to intrude (on)	einfallen
intrusion	Einfall, der
intuition	Anschauung, die
involvement	Sicheinlassen, das
in itself	Ansich, das
journey	Fahrt, die
journeying	Fahren, das
to know also/alongside	mitwissen
to know itself	sich wissen
knowing itself as a self	Sichselbstwissen, das

knowing-itself	Sich-Wissen, das
knowledge, knowing	Wissen
labor	Arbeit, die
lack	Mangel, der
to lay asunder	auseinanderlegen
to lay down	zugrunde legen
laying-itself-asunder	Sichauseinanderlegen, das
laying-open	Aufschließen, das
leap	Sprung, der
leap into	Einsprung, der
leaping attainment	Erspringung, die
letting-appear	Erscheinenlassen, das
letting-arise	Entspringenlassen, das
letting-disappear	Verschwindenlassen, das
letting-emerge	Entstehenlassen, das
letting-itself-show	Sichzeigenlassen, das
to light up	aufleuchten
lighting up	Erleuchten, das
line of sight	Blickrichtung, die
to linger	sich aufhalten
location	Ort, der
looking at	Hinsehen, das
to look out (upon)	hinaussehen (auf)
looking ahead	Voraussehen, das
looking on	Zusehen, das
machination	Machenschaft, die
to make manifest	zur Erscheinung bringen
making room (for)	Einräumung, die
making-present	Vergegenwärtigung, die
manifestation	Manifestation, die; Scheinen, das
manifold	Mannigfaltigkeit, die
matter	Sachverhalt, der
mediatedness	Vermitteltheit, die
mediation	Vermittelung, die
meditation on oneself	Selbstbesinnung, die
meditation	Besinnung, die
mere idea	Einfall, der
mindfulness	Besinnung, die
mood	Stimmung, die
movement	Bewegung, die
need	Not, die
need for decision	Entscheidungsnot, die
negatedness	Verneintheit, die
negating	Negieren, das
negation	Verneinung, die
neglect	Verwahrlosung, die
newness	Neuheit, die

to nihilate	nichten
nihilation	Nichtung, die
non-concept	Unbegriff, der
not-being	Nichtsein, das
not-like	nichthaft
not-ness	Nichtheit, die
null and naught	nichtig
nullity	Nichtigkeit, die
object	Gegenstand, der; Objekt, das
objective	Gegenständliche, das
objectivity	Objektivität, die
objectness	Gegenständlichkeit, die
object-of-consciousness	Bewußte, das
to occur essentially	wesen
to open up	eröffnen
opposition	Gegensatz, der
origin	Ursprung, der
originary	ursprünglich
originary cause	Ur-sache, die
otherness	Andersheit, die
overcoming	Überwindung, die
part of the system	Systemteil, der
particularization	Besonderung, die
passage; passageway	Durchgang, der
passing	Absolvieren, das
passing-over	Übergehen, das
path	Weg, der
peculiar	eigentümlich
perceivedness	Vernommenheit, die
perception	Wahrnehmung, die
permission	Zulassung, die
placing-before	Vor-stellen, das
placing-before-oneself	Vor-sich-stellen, das
point of departure	Ausgang, das
pointing out	Aufzeigen, das
pondering	Bedenken, das
precedence	Voraufgehen, das
pregiven(ness)	Vorgabe, die
pre-possession	Voraus-habe, die
presence	Anwesenheit, die
presencing	Anwesung, die
to present	darstellen
present	Gegenwart, die
present-at-hand	vorhanden
presentation	Darstellung, die
preservation	Aufheben, das
presupposition	Voraussetzung, die

to prevail	walten
previous, prior	voraufgehend
primacy	Vorrang, der
principle	Prinzip, das
procedure	Vorgehen, das
to proceed	ausgehen
process	Vorgang, der
projection	Entwerfen, das; Entwurf, der
proper	eigentlich
to prove (to be), to prove itself	sich erweisen, sich ausweisen, sich herausstellen
to pursue	nachgehen
to push itself to the front	sich vordrängen
question	Frage, die
questionable	fraglich
questionlessness	Fraglosigkeit, die
questionworthy	fragwürdig
to radiate	strahlen
to raise	erheben; hinaufsetzen
to raise up	hinaufheben
ray	Strahl, der
realization	Ausführung, die
realm of inquiry	Fragebereich, der
reflection	Reflexion, die
to refer	beziehen
reflective thinking	Nachdenken, das
refusal	Versagung, die; Verweigerung, die
regard	Hinblick, der; Hinsicht, die
regress	Rückgang, der
to relate	beziehen
relating-itself-to-itself	Sich-auf-sich-selbst-beziehen, das
relation	Bezug, der; Beziehung, die; Verhältnis, das
relationship	Beziehung, die; Bezug, der; Verhältnis, das
release	Loslassen, das; Lossprechung, die
to release itself	sich loslassen
renunciation	Absage, die
representation	Vorstellung, die; Vorstellen, das
representedness	Vorgestelltheit, die
to require	bedürfen
resoluteness	Entschiedenheit, die
to resolve (upon)	beschließen
return	Rückkehr, die
to reveal	offenbaren
reversal	Umkehrung, die
review	Rückblick, der

rule	Herrschaft, die
to run aground	zugrunde gehen
self-appearance	Selbsterscheinen, das
self-assurance	Selbstsicherung, die
self-comprehension	Sichselbstbegreifen, das
self-differentiation	Sichunterscheiden, das
self-evidence	Selbstverständlichkeit, die
self-exposition	Sichdarlegen, das
self-expression	Sichaussprechen, das
self-externalization	Selbstentäußerung,die
self-forgetting	Sichvergessen, das
self-knowledge	Sichwissen, das
self-presentation	Sichdarstellen, das
self-preservation	Sicherhalten, das
self-relevation	Sichoffenbaren, das
self-sameness	Selbigkeit, die
semblance	Schein, der
sense intuition	sinnliche Anschauung, die
sense object	sinnliche Gegenstand, der
separation	Scheiden, das
series	Reihe, die
shape	Gestalt, die
shelter	Schutz, der
shining	Scheinen, das
showing-itself	Sichzeigen, das
sight	Gesicht, das; Sicht, die
singularity	Einzigkeit, die
singularization	Vereinzelung, die
sketch	Entwurf, der
stage	Stufe, die
to stand forth	erstehen
to stand in	innestehen
standing over and against	Entgegenstehen, das
standing together	Zusammenstehen, das
states	Zuständlichkeit, die
step	Schritt, der
stepping forth	Hervortreten, das
structure	Gefüge, das
subject	Subjekt, das
sublation	Aufheben, das
suffering	Erleiden, das
supplement	Nachtrag, der
to supply	herzubringen; hinzubringen
support	Stütze, die
to support	tragen
suspension	Aussetzung, die
synopsis	Zusammensehen, das

synthesis	Synthesis, die
system	System, das; Systematik, die
systematics	Systematik, die
to tackle	zuschaffenmachen; anfallen
to take seriously	Ernst machen (mit)
taking cognizance	Zur-Kenntnis-nehmen
taking notice	Kundnahme, die
taking on	Annehmen, das
taking-upon-oneself	Aufsichnehmen, das
taking up	Aufnehmen, das
to tarry	verweilen; sich aufhalten
tearing	Zerrissenheit, die
the not	Nicht, das
to think in the direction	hinausdenken
thinking-itself	Sich-denken, das
thoughtful, of thought	denkerisch
thoughtfulness	Bedachtsamkeit, die
thoughtness	Gedachtheit, die
thought-provoking	bedenklich
to throw ahead	vorauswerfen
totality	Gesamtheit, die
totality of beings	Seiende im Ganzen, das
traditional	überliefert
transformation	Wandel, der
transition	Übergang, der
transmission	Überlieferung, die
transposedness	Versetztheit, die
traversal	Durchmessen, das
to traverse	durchmessen; durchlaufen
truly, truthfully	wahrhaft
to turn away	abwenden
turnabout	Umwendung, die
turning	Drehung, die; Wendung, die
turning around	Umwendung, die
turning away	Abkehr, die
unconditionally, unconditioned	unbedingt
unconditionedness	Unbedingheit, die
undecidedness	Unentschiedenheit, die
undetermined	unbestimmt
to undergo an experience	Erfahrung machen
underlying	tragend
understanding	Verstand, der
undertaking	Vorhaben, das
undetermined	unbestimmt
unfolding	Entfaltung, die
to unite	einigen
unity	Einheit, die

to venture	wagen
view	Ansicht, die; Blick, der
viewing direction	Blickrichtung, die
way	Bahn, die
to weigh	wägen
what is null and naught	Nichtige, das
what stands against	Gegenstand, der
what truly is a being	wahrhaft Seiende, das
to work through	durcharbeiten
to wreck	zugrunde richten

www.ingramcontent.com/pod-product-compliance
Lightning Source LLC
Chambersburg PA
CBHW030308100426
42812CB00002B/612